THE FARM PROBLEM

THE FARM PROBLEM

The Foundation for Economic Education, Inc.
Irvington-on-Hudson, New York 10533

Published July 1986

ISBN-0-910614-72-5

Copyright © 1986 by

The Foundation for Economic Education, Inc.

Printed in U.S.A.

TABLE OF CONTENTS

Introduction

Down through the ages, countless millions struggling unsuccessfully to keep bare life in wretched bodies, have died young in misery and squalor. Then suddenly, in one spot on this planet, people eat so abundantly that the pangs of hunger are forgotten.

—The Mainspring of Human Progress
HENRY GRADY WEAVER

Such was Weaver's introduction in 1947 to the theme that human liberty is the mainspring of progress and that government tends always to tyranny. He was addressing the problem of food shortage and famine rather than the other side of the coin—the farm problem—stressed in this selection of essays. But food and farming and freedom are so crucially related that they must be considered as a single subject.

"For 60 known centuries," said Weaver, "human beings have gone hungry . . . many have starved." So who is to say precisely where or how "the farm problem" began? But for those of us living in the United States today, the problem generally is said to have begun in the late 1920s and early 1930s when government attempted to do something about it.

The common impression at that time was that the poor farmer was not getting his fair share of the national pie. Therefore, the solution must be to subsidize farmers at taxpayers' expense. After more than a half century of various farm support programs, it becomes increasingly clear that the real problem is the government intervention that distorts and nullifies the price signals of the market place. The consequence of such distortion is an unconscionable burden of expenditures and taxes and unwieldy surpluses of goods artificially priced above the market. In other words, scarce and valuable resources are being wasted on the one hand while human beings still go hungry— and many starve.

The problem is of the sort that calls for freedom as the only solution.

PAUL L. POIROT

Part One

The Problem in Perspective

The United States was founded two centuries ago as a pre-industrial nation. At that time, nine-tenths of the people earned their livelihood in farming. By 1900, about half the labor force worked on the farm. The proportion had shrunk to a fifth of the total by 1940. Today's farm employment accounts for just over three per cent of the civilian labor force.

This is a remarkable account of the growth and development of a nation under a government of limited powers and a comparatively free market. It is characterized not only by an industrial revolution but also by an agricultural revolution. And perhaps more than either of these is the sort of social revolution that accompanies such a mass movement from farm to urban living.

This opening section helps to put the farm problem in perspective through the eyes of Karl Brandt, noted agricultural economist; Clarence Carson with his sharp insights into so many aspects of American history; William Peterson, economist and analyst of *The Great Farm Problem* as reviewed by John Chamberlain in 1959; and a veto message of 1887 by Grover Cleveland explaining why a farm support program would be a mistake.

1

The Hard Core of the Farm Problem

by Karl Brandt

The age-old problem has been to overcome scarcity. So how can it have happened that all of a sudden in the United States there are aggravating surpluses of food and other farm products? There are all sorts of myths and fallacies and supposed explanations—plausibilities that are believed by so many of today's urban dwellers who still have fond memories or nostalgic reverence for the farming experiences of a distant ancestor. These are the issues examined by the late Dr. Karl Brandt, a member of President Eisenhower's Council of Economic Advisers. He had studied the farm problems in several countries as a farm manager, director of an agricultural cooperative and in advisory capacity to governments and international agencies. This article, published in The Freeman *of April 1961, is condensed from an address at the Convention of the Farm Equipment Institute at Dallas, Texas, September 27, 1960.*

For over two thousand years of history, in nearly all countries except our own, the farm problem has been at different times the center of such troubles that bloody revolutions have resulted from it up to this very moment. This problem is today the testing ground for the irreconcilable philosophies that divide this turbulent world, namely, of freedom and respect for human dignity on one side, and atheistic materialism, the coercive economy, and political tyranny on the other. The systems of coercion begin invariably on the farms.

Even more challenging is the fact that in our country, with its peaceful social changes, many years of determined legislative and administrative efforts of the federal government have put us in many ways between the horns of this same old dilemma.

The over-all farm problem in all countries is not a cyclical or temporary affair but is almost eternal in nature and therefore is not amenable to a real remedy or cure. It is part and parcel of the epic of man's struggle for a fuller, more meaningful life. It is composed of continually changing phases of the struggle for survival in, and gradual conquest of, a hostile and scantily yielding nature. It is a story of blood and sweat and toil, of the adventure of defeating the horsemen of the Apocalypse—famine, pestilence, war, and death—which are still stalking the people in many parts of this planet, atom splitting notwithstanding. In all of Christendom this has meant through the centuries a valiant struggle for gaining the material wherewithal for meaningful practice of being kind to thy neighbor, for diminishing poverty, for creating abundance where scarcity and dearth were the common destiny. The farm problem is an integral element in the eternal process economists call economic development and growth.

You may ask whether this is not pretty farfetched in this country with its recurrent problems of too much of too many things, particularly from farm production. My answer is that the emphasis on the combat against the frugality of nature and against adversity comes much closer to the essence of our farm problem than many people realize. Indeed, it is one of the truly unique achievements of the American people, that here on our farms in an environment of freedom and private enterprise they have won the ultimate victory for all nations on this earth in man's battle against the scarcity of food, against hunger and malnutrition, so much so that today any nation can produce an abundance of food, provided its people understand what it takes to do it and are willing to make the proper effort.

Rationale for Planning

What then has happened that had such extraordinary impact on all economic processes? Quite a few people in this country have ready, plausible, yet totally erroneous, answers to this question. If I paraphrase and condense these answers with a little malice toward some, their *leitmotiv* runs like this:

After having taken from the Indians one of the world's richest pieces of a prolifically fertile nature, and having given away a good deal of it for nothing to the railroad magnates and other rugged individualists and ruthless exploiters of natural resources—who in their ghastly greed destroyed with ax and fire millions of acres of beautiful forests and washed into the Mexican Gulf or exported to other exploiters all the nation's heritage of natural fertility of the land—the U.S. government established the Land Grant Colleges, the Agricultural Experiment Stations, and the Extension Service. Thereby the government made farming on what was left over of the eroded and ravished land so productive that it must now proceed to ration all means of production, and control tightly the activities of all the farmers and enforce it by a tough penal code. This must be done particularly because prices are not what they ought to be despite government supports.

This is so because farmers, unlike all other people, are a different breed than all other people, and produce more and more as they progressively get less and less for their products. Measured by some formula of half a century ago, their income is low not only because they maximize their output the lower the prices get, but because all other people in the economy are effectively organized as a conspiracy against the farmer with the labor unions controlling the income of U. S. labor, and the rulers of industries, transportation, and commerce controlling the income of corporations by "administered prices" to the detriment of the farmers in their helpless state of atomistic competition. In view of this effective conspiracy, millions of innocent farm people are driven off the farm by the rascals in all other occupations. Therefore, it is high time for the U. S. government to establish a tight and total control over farm output and guarantee each farmer a just and equitable income. . . .

A Different Interpretation

Let me give you briefly a slightly different view of what in the long run has happened in agriculture's history and what continues to go on in these days. We have ample proof that in Thomas Jefferson's time nine-tenths of the American people earned their livelihood in farming. Around 1900, only 50 per cent of the labor force worked on the farm, and today (1960), less than 10 per cent. This is most significant and illuminating.

What was the state of the U. S. economy then? This can be shown by the economy of many pre-industrial countries which today are still where our economy was 185 years ago. In the underdeveloped economy—except for government personnel, armed forces, teachers, some general stores, and other merchants—nearly all economic activities are carried on at the farm. Food, clothing, shelter, farm and other tools, transportation, education, entertainment, and medication are all produced on the farm. Farmers build houses, barns, and bins in brick, wood, tile, mortar, thatch, and other materials; they lay pavements, dig ditches and canals, build bridges and dams; they raise draft animals, tan hides, and card, spin, and weave wool and fibers; they process and cure any sort of food and bake bread; they slaughter, preserve, smoke, salt, and pickle; they produce wheels and wagons and sleds; and with animal draft power provide transportation on short and long distance with home-built wagons drawn by oxen or cows, horses, donkeys, or mules, camels, or buffaloes, reindeer, or llamas. Farmers provide entertainment at all festivals, nuptials, and after funerals, educate and train the young people, and treat the sick and the aging. So farmers are jacks of all trades, including the production of plants and animals, of lumber and firewood, of peat and gravel and sand, and naval stores. Naturally, what goes to market for cash is little. Hence, it is sheer nonsense to measure their real income in dollars, as it is done today by international agencies for underdeveloped countries. This distorts the true income out of all proportion and serves only to stir resentment against the industrially more advanced nations.

The economy functions in that stage within a structure of total decentralization and with vast numbers of small vertically integrated units. As development begins, one activity after another is segregated from many farms at a time. Hence, not only do new occupations arise, but the skilled workers begin to operate promptly on a much larger scale than before and at much lower costs and prices as well as much higher profits. Many specialized crafts appear: wheelwrights, carriage and harness makers, blacksmiths, and more and more of all the others. Their lower prices expand the market, and their income expands the demand for farm products. If, originally, farmers were jacks of all trades, they gradually became jacks of fewer and fewer trades and thereby more skilled, too. Thus, by the division of labor farm operations become more and more specialized and refined—until ultimately only crops and animals are produced. Gone from the farms are the building trades, the processing of textiles and clothes, the slaughter and curing of meat, until finally even bread, butter, and most other foods are bought because the farm people's time is too precious.

The Complications of Progress

This process of economic development is little understood. It amounts to a piecemeal disassembling and reassembling of the economy with growth of cities and the rise of industries, commerce, transportation, education, research, and a multitude of more and more refined services.

As more people become urban consumers, with a rising purchasing power, they are bidding not for more calories, but for a diet with more calories from products with a high value added such as sugar, milk, meat, bacon, butter, eggs, fruits, and vegetables, and less from starchy staples like corn, wheat, and potatoes. With a rising demand for their products in the markets the people remaining on the farm increase their output, and with it their productivity and income. In order to do this, they have to equip themselves with better tools, more mechanical power, better plants and animals. In other words, they must increase the capital at their command, and must perform with ever-increasing efficiency as farm managers and workers.

All of this is proceeding every day in our decentralized free enterprise economy where people are not pushed from one job to another by the government or anybody else, but where they make their own choice and choose their occupation, their place of work and living, according to their own preference and the available opportunities. In doing this the families evaluate the whole package of working and living conditions, the opportunity of improving their composite income in cash, kind, and amenities, the security of their job and livelihood. Even in the backwoods they usually know very well what other jobs pay, and they decide to take or leave the often better pay.

He who claims that in recent years several million farm people "have been driven off the farm" has to explain first who was responsible for the shift from 90 per cent to 10 per cent from farm to nonfarm work in 185 years. Who drove them off? The answer is: nobody, except perhaps occasionally a nagging partner in marriage. Those who left did the sensible thing to contribute their service where it was needed most as the country developed and the economy started and continued to grow. In our system of free people nobody has a right to determine where the people live and where they work on what, except they themselves. In fact, so long as they ask for no support from us, pay their taxes, and are not delinquent as parents of minor children, we have no right to force them to be efficient or to increase their income, even if they prefer to live like a hermit or to sleep like Rip Van Winkle.

Growth Involves Change

It is axiomatic that without the movement of people from farms to towns and cities, all industrial and urban development—the entire construction of a civilization on a continent that 100 years ago was still mostly wilderness—would have been impossible.

Moreover, in this long historical shift from farms to urban life and work lies the key to the secret in all modern democracies which puzzles even political scientists and which few people understand: namely, the fact that the smaller the proportion of farm people in the electorate, the more they are assured of the good will of urban voters, legislators, and administrators and their readiness to grant farm aid. It is not the political power of a farm bloc that guarantees this, but the subconscious memory of all people in Western industrial society that all of them originally came from the farm which solidly anchors their fondness and affection for the farm people. I call this the urban dwellers' image of "Paradise Lost": the farm as the forebears' origin and the happy valley where life is imagined as having been simple, safe, harmonious, and peaceful. Mixed into such nostalgia is a feeling of guilt toward those who were left behind in the heroic march of urban progress and are condemned to live in social isolation, forced to do hard physical work for long hours, being tied to tend to cows and other animals 365 days, exposed to the vicissitudes and hazards of weather and unstable international markets. Hence, the urban voters have nothing against subsidies for the poor fellows on the farm, even if it means many billions of taxpayers' money.

Irrespective of how far these thoughts are from reality, they are anchored deep in the nation's soul. Fortunately, what has actually happened on the farms is far more complex than the average citizen can realize and the situation there is quite different from such nostalgic sentiments.

Our economy has grown in the long run at a very steady rate, and this growth has at all times been hinged to the rise in agricultural productivity, meaning the rate of output per man-hour. In recent years the rate of productivity gain on farms has not only left the population growth and the growth per capita income way behind, but also the rate of productivity gain in the rest of the economy.

Agriculture is in reality the world's oldest and greatest industry of year-round transportation. In this country (1960) our presently four million farms use and operate 470 million acres of cropland, and 900 million acres of grazing land, or a total of 1,370,000,000 acres from below sea level to high mountain plateaus. On the cropland every square foot has to be worked or passed with implements and tools, or loads of materials many times every year—indeed, for some crops up to 35 times—and where double or triple cropping takes place, even more often. And people and livestock and bulky commodities have to be transported from town to farm and from farm to town.

Therefore, to a large extent the saga of progress on the farm is the saga of the fabulous evolution in the technology of transportation. The American Indians had no domesticated animals, no ox, no donkey, no horse, and not even a cart with wheels. The Spaniards brought cattle, donkeys, mules, horses, and wagons; and other colonial powers to whom we owe our origin and early success brought more of them. From their beginning, American farmers, with the employment of ultimately over 30 million draft animals, took up to the beginning of this century some 450 million acres of cropland and some 700 million acres of grazing land into agricultural use and cleared in the process some 400 million acres of forest land with its moist soils. This cost three generations of gruesome toil, a piece of homework Soviet Russia still has to do in the future. But contrary to the ignorant indictment by politicians in the early thirties, this clearing of the woodland was one of the great achievements on which the European civilization was built also.

As the economy developed, draft animals became clearly too inefficient in use of both cropland and manpower. Labor, especially, was too scarce and expensive to be wasted. In this century at long last, the internal combustion engine became the effective replacement to animal power—though first, and still predominantly, in this country. It provided individual motive power for the totally decentralized transportation industry that happens to be identical with agriculture. Progress was slow and halting; you could replace the horse only by the combination of three motor vehicles: the tractor, the truck, and the car, because the horse had four or more gears. As oxen, horses, and mules were replaced, mineral fuel set free over 50 million acres of cropland and additional grazing land for other livestock and crops.

Mechanical Power

Today (1960) we have a fleet of 15 million tractors, trucks, cars, and combines, plus many millions of electric motors on less than four million farms. A recent estimate listed the mechanical power equipment of our farms at 115.6 million horsepower, all factories at 28.2 million horsepower and all railroads at 88.7 million horsepower. The result is a gigantic increase in all transportation on the farm while transportation off the farm has mostly been taken over by others. With oxen, horses, and mules practically gone, there is more speed, more power, more versatility for the manpower on farms, having set free so much of it that, for decades to come, less will be needed to feed a rapidly growing population.

The value of the equipment of our farms including machinery and motor vehicles has increased in the last 20 years from $3 billion to over $18 billion current dollars, but in terms of work capacity and actual performance, immeasurably more. Of course, farmers buy more new machinery, not because they are new gadgets or do more fancy stunts, but only and exclusively if, and when, all costs per unit of work leave a clear net gain over the costs replaced.

Improved Production Methods

Simultaneous with the vigorous mechanization, the production per plant and per acre of crops and per animal unit has been increased. Crop yields were boosted by better cultural practices, improved seed, more efficient protection of plants against weeds, rodents, insects, worms, bacteria, and fungi, but first and last of all, by better feeding of the plants with more nutrients. Among the nutrients, the key factor turned out to be *nitrogen*. This vital element in the life-bearing proteins is mined with energy from the air by the world's biggest nitrogen producing industry in this country, where it serves as fertilizer, rocket propellant, and base for chemicals. And since plants fed with more nitrogen have rapidly increasing moisture requirements and burn up if they run short of it, farmers applied more supplementary irrigation to break this bottleneck. According to European experience, one ton of nitrogen produces 15 to 20 tons of grain equivalent. Our farm application of nitrogen has increased from next to zero in prewar years to over two million tons, while simultaneously sprinkler irrigation has spread into all states of the Union including the humid ones up to Maine. This was due to the decline in the price of aluminum pipe and motor pump units. The economic force that pushed this acceptance of better technology was again the increasing spread between the costs per unit of nutrient of water applied to the crop and the price per unit of product produced with it.

For animal husbandry the same has happened. Animals are only converters of feed. If one could produce cheaper feed by putting nitrogen in irrigated pastures, he could produce milk or beef at lower cost, and with more profit if the price did not drop too much. But in addition, hybridization, antibiotics, better feed mixtures, and other methods have helped to improve the input-output ratios.

The aggregate impact of all this increased productivity is enormous and has become the envy of the world. With their unique managerial talents, their up-to-date equipment, and the unequaled services provided by the enterprises and institutions of the rest of the economy, the American farmers have developed their giant business to the greatest chemical industry in the world, that of converting annually 280 million tons of roughage, succulent feed, and concentrates, plus a million acres of grazing forage, to animal products. This is capitalism at its best, with the able capitalists in overalls on the tractors, or hay-balers, or in the mechanical milking parlor. Many people do not know it, but if government payments and surplus purchases are excluded, U. S. farms (1960) earn $19 billion, or way over 60 per cent of their cash receipts, from sales of livestock products. This is done with over 170 million grain-consuming animal units and close to 100 million roughage-consuming animal units, or as much "capital on the hoof" in live inventories as there is in machinery inventory, namely, $18 billion in each. This is one of the secrets of success of U. S. agriculture's productivity: it has the capital, which it can depreciate, maintain, or expand. In the Soviet orbit and many other countries of the world the rulers squeeze every penny of capital out of agriculture in order to invest it in publicly-owned industries, to the consequence of low productivity and waste of natural resources. The greatest farm income support is rapid depreciation allowance for farm machinery and breeding stock under the revenue code.

American vs. Russian Output

Let me sum up what this huge business of agriculture amounts to in terms of output (1960). It produces in a year with no more than 8.5 per cent of the national labor force, or 7.4 million workers, over *200 million tons of grain, 3 million tons of sugar, over 20 million tons of meat and eggs, over 60 million tons of milk, 35 million tons of fruit and vegetables, or 315 million tons of edible products*, plus *3.5 million tons of cotton*, and *nearly 1 million tons of tobacco*. In order to measure the magnitude of these figures I mention that after 40 years of a brutal experiment of collectivization, Soviet Russia produces with 4½ times the number of farm workers (33 million) one-third as much meat (7 million tons) as do our farmers; and even of grain, most of which they eat rather than feed to livestock, they produce only 60 per cent as much as our output. This in spite of an abundance of natural resources in Europe and Asia. One American farmer produces food for himself and 24 others. A Soviet farmer produces enough for himself and 4 others.

Interference with Markets

Where then lies the hard core of our farm problem? What I have shown is that while the urban people left behind what in restrospect sometimes looks like a lost paradise, but was in reality an enormous amount of sweat and toil, of drudgery and disease, our agriculture of today is an extremely dynamic business world of its own. The government has called it into action in two world wars and then for the first war of the UN, that in Korea. In the three instances an assignment of all-out production was achieved with guaranteed high prices. But when the aftermath of World War I led to deflation and later the great industrial depression, the Congress adopted a policy of farm income support in which fixed prices were maintained by government purchase and disposal at a loss, combined with acreage allotments and, in some cases, marketing quotas.

Since the support prices were deliberately set above the equilibrium level at which demand would equal supply and since the government made an open-end commitment to buy all that the market would not absorb, the farmers responded generously to the incentive. The allotment control was defeated by intensification, i.e, by higher input. The marketing quotas were defeated as control measures by shifting the surplus to other commodities. Our farm legislation has about the same effect as if someone had jimmied the voting machine on which the consumers could vote for what farm products they wanted, and how much of them. In other words, the price signals are out of commission.

Of the four million farms (1960), roughly two million full-fledged commercial units produce some 93 per cent of the marketed product. They have some adjustment problems for a few commodities, particularly wheat, but are not in any financial or income calamity. In fact, their business is by any standard relatively satisfactory, especially if we look at the regular and substantial gain accruing in their equity. These farms are one of the greatest assets this nation has and its technology is the greatest asset of the West.

But we have serious problems among certain groups of the remaining two million small, so-called low income farms, particularly in some retarded areas like the Appalachians, the Piedmont, the Ozarks, and in the reforestation areas of the upper Lake States. In general the two million small farms need outside employment, mixing nonfarm and farm incomes. No one suggests their abandonment as living quarters. It would be a serious mistake, however, to lump the two million heterogeneous units as suffering alike from too-small incomes. A large part of these are retirement and part-time farms which offer a most desirable form of rural existence for people who have a security insured by pensions, tax benefits, and a flow of part-time work income. The number of this type of farm will grow in the future. They constitute no social or economic problem.

Jobs in Town

There are other farms where the people must avail themselves of the nearby educational and training facilities to find better employment for their young people. It still remains true that only the people themselves can make the decision to move, to change to other occupations, or to undertake better farming practices. Indeed, they are on their way. While farm operators earned $11.8 billion net income from farming last year (1959), the total farm population earned an additional $8.5 million net income from farm work off the farm and from nonagricultural sources.

There is a serious legislative farm problem, definitely not an administrative one. Our farms are by and large in fairly good health, ready to feed 200-, 250-, or 300 million Americans in the future, and better than ever. The real farm problem concerns the question as to how one can liberate the Treasury from the burden of an impossible open-end commitment and a continuous misinvestment in more and more grain without doing harm to the farm community and all those who serve it. This disengagement from faulty legislation requires common sense, a warm heart, and a cool head. It requires an honest businesslike approach and due respect for the basic institutions on which the American economy stands or falls and for the true stature of the farm business with its more than $200 billion productive assets (1960).

We have out-produced the Soviets many times over and have all the benefits of our productivity, but we cannot borrow from them a compulsory production control system which involves the cartelization of agriculture and all farm supply industries without ruining our prosperous farming system. There are two ways of becoming Sovietized: by conquest or subversion is one, by voluntary assimilation of their institutions is the other.

Unfortunately, we have in our midst too many self-styled friends of the farmers who know exactly what is good for other people and are yearning to wield just enough power to prescribe from some office desk the recipe for the social medicine the people have to swallow and the orders as to what they have to do or not do. For my taste there is too much affluency in telling the farmers and their suppliers what to do and telling the customers what not to spend their money on.

If we fall for giving these people too much leeway, they will go at it and try to take the competitiveness out of our agriculture and with it its creative dynamic quality. If I were farming right now, I would be tempted to say in these coming weeks every now and then a silent prayer: Good Lord, protect me from my friends; against my enemies I can defend myself.

2

The Trouble With Farming

by Clarence B. Carson

Dr. Clarence Carson's roots lead back to his boyhood on a farm in Alabama, a countryside then dotted with houses of small landowners, tenants, and dwellings for hired laborers. Now those relics of a simpler life are gone. And as a skilled student and teacher of American history, in all its aspects, Dr. Carson examines this change with special reference to cotton growing in the Mississippi Delta and the consequences of price supports, loan programs, and other aspects of our age of inflation.

Dr. Carson has written extensively for The Freeman, *this article having appeared in May 1983. The most recent in his long list of books is the five-volume series,* A Basic History of the United States.

This past December, I traveled with my family through north central Mississippi and across the river northwestward into south central Arkansas. The portion of the trip that made the deepest impression on me was that which took us through what is called the Mississippi Delta.

The Delta stretches for the better part of 100 miles inland on either side of the Mississippi river in this area, though somewhat wider on the Mississippi than the Arkansas side. The land is table flat, and the road we were on was arrow straight, bending only so much as was necessary to put it through the next town. The road was raised three or four feet above the surrounding countryside, which was fortunate for us. The countryside was flooded by unusually heavy winter rains, and the flooding was enhanced by a blinding rain squall as we drove through one of the more remote regions. When the ground is too full to soak up the water, there is no place handy for it to go.

This is farming country, though it was dormant at this season. More, it is row-crop farming country. Few, if any, cattle or hogs were to be seen, and woodland was rare. Twenty-five or thirty years ago, it was predominantly cotton country. Cotton is still grown extensively—many stalks were still standing, with traces of lint hanging from the empty bolls—but the growing of grains, especially soybeans, has widely supplanted cotton.

The Mississippi Delta belongs geographically to a much vaster farming region, extending from Minnesota in the north to Louisiana in the south and from western Ohio in the east to eastern Colorado in the west. It is a vast fertile region, much of it low lying to flat country with deep soil, well-suited in this age to commercial farming.

It is the Mississippi valley, the low lying area through which the waters which begin in the western Appalachians and the eastern Rockies flow into the Mississippi, and thence to the sea. The region of the valley narrows from north to south as the mountains recede in height and fan out into foothills which channel the water along other courses to the Gulf of Mexico. The Mississippi valley is sometimes called the heartland of America. It is certainly the breadbasket, for most of the grain that feeds America is grown there.

The Mississippi Delta through which I traveled has undergone a major change in the past two or three decades, a change that was very nearly completed by 1970, say. Although vast acreages of land are under cultivation now, the country is sparsely inhabited. Houses are usually located a considerable distance from one another; often, they are separated by a mile, or more, of farmland. Usually, a single family dwelling sits alone, with the mechanical equipment for farming nearby.

An Agricultural Revolution

Twenty-five or thirty years ago it would not have been possible for such a small number of farmers to till these great acreages. This Mississippi Delta was one of the major centers of cotton growing in the United States. Cotton required intensive cultivation—it had to be hoed several times by hand—and many human hands to harvest any considerable amount of it. Two major developments altered these requirements. One was the development of herbicides to get rid of unwanted weeds and grass. The other was the development of a mechanical cotton picker. Along with this, there was increasing use of mechanical planters and fertilizer distributors which could be extended across a wide carrying frame to plant many rows. There also were larger cultivators. The reduction of hands used was further accelerated in the 1960s by the extension of the minimum wage to cover farm laborers.

So it is that a countryside once dotted with houses of small landowners, tenants, and dwellings for hired laborers is now sparsely settled by farmers who rely almost exclusively upon heavy equipment to do the work. I looked in vain for relics of these buildings. I noted none. There were reports in the 1960s that they were burned to be rid of them.

A similar change or transformation has occurred in farming throughout the

United States, though less dramatic than in cotton farming in most instances. Here and there are still enclaves of farming which require intensive human care and human hands and decisions in harvesting, such as in tobacco growing or in the production and harvesting of some fruits and vegetables. By and large, though, the extensive use of machines, the shift away from intensive use of labor, and the cultivation of large acreages by single farm families has been the trend throughout most of American agriculture.

Fewer Farms—and Farmers

Statistics tell much of the story in abstract terms. According to census figures, the total number of farms in the United States has declined from 6,102,000 in 1940 to 2,808,000 in 1980. The most drastic decline for any decade was in the 1950s, when the number of farms dropped from 5,388,000 in 1950 to 3,962,000 in 1960. The number of farms appears to have stabilized over the past decade or so.

The total farm population declined from 30,547,000 in 1940 to 8,864,000 in 1980. Again, the largest drop in farm population occurred in the 1950s, when it declined from 23,048,000 in 1950 to 15,635,000 in 1960. The number of hired farm workers (average) in 1920 was 3,391,000; in 1940, 2,679,000; in 1980, 1,303,000. The largest drop in hired farm workers occurred in the 1960s, which coincides with the application of the minimum wage to them. Farms have been increasing in size over the same period, of course, and it might go without saying that they have generally been increasing precipitately in value.

The main conclusion to be drawn from these facts is that fewer and fewer people are farming more and more land (per farmer) by the use of more and more equipment. Or, in formal economic terms, there has been a dramatic shift away from labor in the economic mix to land and capital, especially capital.

Moreover, not only are fewer people farming more land with more equipment, but also they are producing more of many commodities than ever before. For example, here is a description of production in 1981:

> The corn crop of 8,080,000,000 bushels, or 205 million metric tons (t), was the largest on record and 22% greater than the 1980 crop. All feed grain production . . . was 240 million t, up 21% from . . . 1980. Also the soybean crop of 2,110,000,000 bushels was the second largest crop on record and . . . 18% larger than the 1980 crop. The U. S. wheat crop was a record 2,750,000,000 bushels . . . , 377 million bushels more than in 1980. Cotton production of 14.8 million bales was 33% greater than in 1980. Hay production increased 5% over 1980, while pasture and range conditions were 22% better than in 1980. Due to lower livestock prices during the first half of 1980, the number of hogs raised, the number of

cattle fed for beef, and the number of chickens raised were down slightly. (*American Annual* [Grolier, 1982], p. 78)

The production achieved by American farmers by way of this heady shift to capital is surely little short of being one of the wonders of the modern world. Moreover, the prices of farm products to consumers should generally be reckoned as a bargain, compared to the prices of many other goods in an era of rising prices.

Signs of Distress

But there is a rather large worm in the apple of this farming Eden, which brings us to the subject of this essay, the trouble with farming. Discontent among farmers has been widespread and, perhaps, increasingly strident in recent years. There have been tractorcades to some state capitals and to the national capital, confrontations with sheriffs at foreclosure sales, and dark threats of violence if something is not done to help farmers.

The most common complaint is that farm prices are so low that large numbers of farmers cannot make ends meet. Stories surface after each crop year of farmers who lost large sums of money. Nor are the difficulties restricted to farmers in any one section of the country or producers of particular farm goods. They range from dairy farmers to chicken and egg producers to grain and fiber farmers to cattle growers.

Farmers are not noted, of course, for boasting about their great profits. Who is? Those who work and produce rarely complain that they are overpaid or admit that they are adequately compensated for their efforts. It could be, too, that when farmers gather in the winter, bragging rights sometimes belong to the farmer who had the largest losses during the year. But there is naught of exaggeration or humor in the inability of farmers to make payments on their debts or the ensuing bankruptcies and foreclosures. These last are widespread and increasing by all accounts. Moreover, precipitately mounting farmer indebtedness signifies something of the extent of the difficulties.

Total farm real estate debt outstanding stood at slightly over $7 billion in 1953. At the end of 1981, it stood at over $92 billion. There was a steady, though not particularly dramatic, rise in farm real estate debt during the 1950s and 1960s. It began taking off in the 1970s and almost doubled between 1975 and 1981. Closer analysis shows, too, that the least well secured—most precarious— portion of the indebtedness was increasing even more rapidly. Indebtedness to the Farmer's Home Administration, the lender of last resort for farmers, almost doubled in the period 1979–1981. These figures do not include the indebtedness for shorter terms secured by farm equipment or "rollover" debts, not completely retired from year to year because the proceeds from the sale of produce were insufficient. These add substantially to the overall debt.

Contributing Factors

A good many contributory reasons can be enumerated for short-term difficulties of farmers in general and those of individual farmers here and there in particular. Most likely, some farmers who go bankrupt or have their farms foreclosed are ineffective managers. Some are what economists call marginal, or on their way to becoming sub-marginal, farmers.

More broadly, there have been fluctuations and changes which had an impact on farmers generally. One was the oil embargo of the Arab countries and the subsequent steep rise in oil prices. This development not only drove fuel prices up but also the prices of such things as fertilizer, pesticides, and herbicides. Another development has been the sharp rise in interest rates in recent years. Embargoes on grain shipments to communist countries have aggravated the situation for grain growers also. It can be added that, of course, farming is a risky business, and the vagaries of weather, of pests, and diseases contribute to the fluctuations in farm production.

These, and like, explanations might suffice if the trouble with farming were temporary or episodic. But some of the signs, especially mounting indebtedness, point to persistent and increasing difficulty. Moreover, if it were simply a market phenomenon, we might expect that farmers would make the necessary adjustments of production to demand to get prices that would enable those who stayed in the business to prosper. But it is not simply a market phenomenon, certainly not of the free market anyway. None of the developments discussed above were simply responses to the free market: not the dramatic shift from extensive labor toward capital, not the enlargement of farms, not the buying of ever larger and more expensive farm equipment, not the mounting indebtedness.

All these occurred in a framework of government tampering, intervention, restriction, subsidization, and tacit inducement. Farmers have been propelled, as it were, in the direction they have taken, including producing more than could be profitably sold, by government programs over the years. That is not to say that some of the developments, such as the shift toward capital by the use of large and specialized machines, would not have taken place, sooner or later, without the intervention. But it is most unlikely that the changes would have occurred so swiftly, so dramatically, or so extensively if the market had been the sole prompter of them. That is a way of saying that it is most unlikely that farmers would have been caught in their present bind by the workings of a free market. At any rate, that is *not* the way it happened.

Although there have been many government programs over the years which affected farming more or less in a variety of ways, I want to focus on three categories of programs which have the most direct bearing on the present situation. They are price supports, crop and production restrictions, and easy credit. While easy credit is at the heart of the present farmer difficulties, other programs provide an essential part of the background and highlight some of the fallacies which underlie them.

Price Supports

Farmers have long and often believed that their problems, when they became acute, were caused by low prices for their production. Over the past century, they, or those who claimed to speak for them, have identified a number of villains who either contributed to or caused the low prices. Among these were high transportation costs, extortionate rates for storage facilities, money shortage, the fact that farmers often sold their crops at the time when prices were lowest, protective tariffs on manufactured goods, middleman profits, and, belatedly and occasionally, their own overproduction. Coupled with this has been a sentimental attitude toward farmers and farming, which goes back at least to Thomas Jefferson and was vigorously intruded into the political scene by William Jennings Bryan in the late 1890s. There were sporadic political attempts to "aid" the farmer by making easier money available and regulating rail rates over the years.

However, it was not until the 1930s that the federal government made a concerted effort to raise farm prices. The New Deal devised a variety of programs designed to accomplish this result. Among them were programs to increase the money supply, make loans on crops stored in warehouses until prices rose, subsidies, government guarantees, and government bidding up of prices. Some one, combination, or all of these efforts did succeed in raising farm prices, or some of them.

It happens, however, that one of the most important economic functions of price is to signal what is wanted. Higher farm prices tend to spur farmers to produce more of the goods for which prices are rising. (Not all farm products had price supports.) If the New Dealers did not know this at the beginning, there would soon be bountiful evidence to prove it. In any case, they were intent on raising prices, and they did understand that the way to do that was to reduce the supply on the market. Sometimes, they, or their successors in government, limited the amount of particular crops that could be sold at support prices. But the main device by which government tried to limit production over the years was by acreage restrictions on controlled crops. Farmers were assigned crop allotments for crops that had price supports, usually for their commercial or "money" crops.

Distorted Signals

The combination of price supports and acreage (or production) restrictions bent or distorted the market in opposite directions. On the one hand, price supports, so far as they succeeded in raising prices above what they would have been on the market, signaled farmers to increase production. On the other hand, acreage allotments limited the amount of land that could be planted to those crops. That did not mean that farmers gave up in their efforts to increase production of supported crops. It did mean, however, that they would have to shift the economic mix from labor toward capital. In theory, they might have cultivated the commercial supported crops more intensely in the hope of increasing production. But that was hardly possible, even if it would have worked.

The government program was set up in a way that discouraged the concentration of labor on the controlled crop. Allotments were based on the total amount of land under cultivation on a given farm. (Government favored diversified farming.) Thus, on a farm, only an established percentage of the land could be planted to the controlled crop. In order to get his maximum allotment, a farmer had to keep a maximum amount of his land in cultivation. He could, of course, concentrate his capital expenditures for fertilizer, improved seeds, pesticides, and the like, on the commercial and controlled crops. Many, probably most, farmers did. More, when they could, farmers increased their capital expenditures for these over what they had done, for it was a route to increasing production.

Beyond that, however, farmers who survived generally had to bring more land under cultivation, rent it or buy it (or buy allotments, as was sometimes done in the 1950s and 1960s) to make a living. The record is clear that most of those on small farms could not make a go of farming. The mass exodus from farming got under way in earnest in the mid-1930s and continued to the late 1960s, when farm population tended to stabilize. The main path taken by farmers was to increase farm holdings. Since the number of hired farm workers was generally declining during this period, the main approach taken to the cultivation of these larger acreages was to buy mechanical farm equipment, i.e., tractors, trucks, planters, cultivators, and harvesters. Thus, the shift from labor toward capital was completed, so far as it has been.

From Whence the Capital?

Where did the farmers get the capital? More bluntly, where did they get the money to buy the machines, the fertilizer, the pesticides, the herbicides, the improved seeds, irrigation systems, and the like? In addition, where did they get the money to buy or rent additional land? There is no need to generalize too broadly here.

Most likely, there have been farmers who financed their expansion over the years in a businesslike and sound financial way. They extended their land holdings from profits, savings, inheritances, and so forth, and bought additional land only as it became available at attractive prices. Such people might well have bought new and larger equipment from similar sources, supplemented by prudent borrowing. If so, and if they have managed well, they are probably succeeding in farming even today. In any case, we are looking for the sources of the difficulties of farmers in trouble. More, we are looking for what, in addition to support prices, has enabled farmers to get the capital to produce in such quantity that they cannot survive in farming with such price supports as still exist.

The source of much of the money for farm capital and land is no great mystery. It has been borrowed. It has been made available by *easy credit*. The easy credit is a result of the policies and programs of the United States government. The farm movement that got underway in the latter part of the nineteenth century was early penetrated with the idea that easy money, or inflation, was a panacea for the problems of farmers.

This easy-credit idea achieved political expression in the Greenbacker and silverite movement, was propounded by the Populists in the 1890s, and entered the Democratic party by way of William Jennings Bryan and his followers in 1896. It began to bear fruit when the next Democrat, Woodrow Wilson, was elected to the presidency in 1912. The Federal Reserve Act was passed in 1913. The banks authorized under it were to become engines of inflation, for they were empowered to issue currency on the security of commercial and *agricultural* paper. That is, they could expand the credit by rediscounting notes held by banks, thus making more money and credit available.

The Federal Reserve System, then, has been the main fount of easy credit in the United States generally since that time. It is important to emphasize, however, that farm credit is a breed all its own. Otherwise, it might be supposed that farm financing is done in the same way as for other businesses. True, commerical farming is a business, and farm enterprises are often referred to as agribusiness. But much of farm financing is not done under such restraints as apply to business concerns. Farming is an especially risky business, yet much of the risk capital is obtained as loans rather than from investors who knowingly share in the risk. Also, much of farm land is financed by borrowing.

The Farm Credit System

How has this come about? Mainly by the operation of what has come to be called the Farm Credit System. Since little is known about this system generally, and since those who know of one or more of its agencies may not be aware of the government connections or the strange organizational modes, some little explanation of it may be in order.

First, the Farm Credit System was government inspired, government authorized, had had initial and occasional government financial help, and is government controlled! The basic system was authorized by the Federal Farm Loan Act of 1916. The Federal Land Banks, probably the best known of the organizations, were first organized in 1917, pursuant to this act. There have been changes in the system from time to time by congressional acts. The following remarks are about the system as it was authorized by the Farm Credit Act of 1971.

According to the U.S. Government *Manual*, the system is organized in this way:

> The Farm Credit Administration, an independent agency, supervises and coordinates activities of the cooperative Farm Credit System. The system is comprised of Federal land banks and Federal land bank associations, Federal intermediate credit banks and production credit associations, banks for cooperatives. Initially capitalized by the United States, the entire System is now owned by its users.

Some of the above information could be misleading, however. The Farm Credit Administration is "independent" in the sense that it does not fall under the authority of any regular department of the government. Otherwise, it is a government agency, as are all the others under its authority, and the governing board is politically appointed: 12 members by the President of the United States and one by the Secretary of Agriculture.

This is a nationwide system of credit for farmers, the central banks being distributed about over the country in much the same way as are Federal Reserve banks. The Federal Land Banks make long term (5 to 40 year) loans to farmers secured by real estate. Although portions of the loans may be used for other purposes, they are made basically for the acquisition of farm land. The Intermediate Credit Banks are discount banks, serving mainly Production Credit Associations. Their main purpose is to discount intermediate term notes, such as would be needed for the purchase of farm equipment. Production Credit Associations make mainly what should be called risk capital loans to farmers. The loans may be for periods of up to 7 years. Banks for Cooperatives are, as the name implies, banks for associations of farmers.

Specialized Loan Companies

None of these organizations are banks in the usual meaning of the term. They are neither depositories of money nor issuers of currency. They might better be called loan companies, for that is their function, loan companies established by the United States government. But the word "company" may be misleading, if by that term we mean an organization owned and operated by investors for profit. The organizations in the Farm Credit System do not fit that description. The investors have no control over the organizations; investment is separated from ownership; hired managers operate them; and the profits, if any, go to the borrowers. Basic policy is set by political appointees or by law. Financing came initially from the Federal government, and ongoing financing comes from consolidated bonds sold to investors and backed by the notes from borrowers. (The United States government does not guarantee these bonds, but that may be only a technicality.)

The borrowers hold the voting stock in the basic organizations for the duration of their indebtedness. They are required to purchase the stock in order to obtain loans, and when the loans are repaid they must either relinquish the stock, or, in some cases, accept non-voting stock in return. The voting stock serves basically as a means of choosing the members of the committee which approves or disapproves loans. Such profits as may be made are, in effect, paid out as reductions of interest rates to current borrowers.

The point of these arrangements may be easier to get by conceiving the matter in figurative language. The government has contrived to bring into being and caused to be planted and grown a vast cabbage patch, i.e., credit, for rabbits, i.e., farmers. The rabbits have been placed in charge of distributing the cabbages under guidelines laid down by politicians or their appointees. My point is that a vast system of easy credit to enable farmers to buy land and get risk capital has been made available by government. But to round out the account of credit institutions one more needs to be included. It is the Farmer's Home Administration (known as the F.H.A. in rural circles).

The F.H.A.

The Farmer's Home Administration is a backup organization to provide easy credit, mainly for farmers, who cannot meet the requirements of other lenders. (Applicants for loans are usually expected to submit evidence that they have been turned down by other lending institutions.) Its basic authority stems from an act of Congress passed in 1921. It operates within the Department of Agriculture, and it is financed by proceeds from the sale of Treasury certificates. It makes loans to "pay for equipment, livestock, feed, seed, fertilizer, other farm and home operating needs; refinance chattel debts; provide operating credit to fish farmers;" for the purchase of land, houses, and other sorts of things for rural inhabitants and farmers. Terms of repayment and interest rates are adjusted to the financial situation of the borrowers.

None of this is meant to suggest that farmers borrow exclusively from government agencies. They, or some of them at least, borrow from regular banks, from insurance companies, from equipment dealers, and from private as well as other public sources. But there is every reason to believe that the major source of the easy credit which has many of them now swamped with debts are the government agencies.

While I was in the midst of writing this article there was an account on television of a farmer in Ohio who was trying to prevent the auctioning of his farm to pay his debts, or at least those secured by it. According to the television announcer, the man had 199 acres of land, and he owed $400,000 to a Production Credit Association and $200,000 to a Federal Land Bank.

Much more generally, the breakdown of the lenders to whom were owed the more than $92 billion outstanding farm real estate debt in 1981 confirms the preponderance of these agencies. The largest portion, nearly $36 billion, is owed to the Federal Land banks. Nearly $8 billion is owed to the Farmer's Home Administration. Life insurance companies had loaned nearly $13 billion, and commercial banks somewhat under $9 billion. The other lenders were not enumerated.

Here is a synopsis of an Associated Press release (published in the Birmingham *News*, January 2, 1983, p. 21A) which illustrates the ease with which farmers could borrow money and the consequences of debt for one man. It is about a man who was a farmer in Missouri. He began farming in 1965 with 68 acres of land and $600. By 1970, he was planting 900 acres and feeding several hundred hogs. This expansion was built upon a mountain of debt; it eventually totaled nearly $400,000. Drought, a disease which decimated his hog population, and inadequate prices drove him to the wall. The Production Credit Association, which had been supplying the risk capital for his operation, could carry him no longer. He turned to the Farmer's Home Administration, but that aid did not last long. His farm was sold at auction, but many of the debts remain unpaid.

In retrospect, this farmer understands what happened to him this way. He believes

> he still would be farming had he not expanded with such zeal. Had his appetite for money not been so voracious. Had that money not been dished out so readily.
> "They made a feather bed for me to lie on . . . ," [he] said of the lenders.
> "You know, I could basically sit down at my kitchen table and write out a loan. It was just too simple."

"The road to hell," it has been said, "is paved with good intentions." The road to trial and tribulation for farmers is paved with government programs. Undoubtedly, farmers would have a full quota of trouble if there were no government intervention. Commercial farming is a business, and it is beset with all the pitfalls of other businesses. Some businesses prosper, others fail. That is the story of all business in good times and bad, and especially in bad. Beyond that, farmers face some risks peculiar to their undertaking. Thus, however unfortunate it may be, farming is unlikely ever to be a universally prospering undertaking for all who venture into it.

Conclusions

But the conclusions toward which this article has been moving are these. Government intervention has greatly aggravated the lot of the farmers. Price supports induce farmers to produce more. That, plus crop restrictions, promoted the expansion of land holdings and the shift from labor toward capital. Despite the fact that this was risk capital, the government set up a vast credit mechanism to supply much of it.

Price supports, crop restrictions, and easy credit sent misleading signals into the market. The crop restrictions have generally been abandoned over the past couple of decades, not, however, before millions of people had been driven from farming and the pattern had been set for those who remained to expand their land holdings and rely more and more on capital. Price supports, while not so obtrusive as they once were, still serve to stimulate production. Meanwhile, farmers go deeper and deeper in debt in a desperate effort to produce more and more in the hope that they can pay off the debts which are threatening to crush them. Many are falling by the way. Others, perhaps most, are having a hard time due to the lower prices resulting from the increasing production.

Many farmers are raising the cry for government aid once again. But the hair of the dog that bit them will no more solve their problems than it will cure alcoholism. Neither economic theory nor historical experience supports any such notion. It is government intervention which has bent, strained and distorted the market to produce the current mess, as well as a number of earlier ones.

The unhampered market provides the guides for how much to produce in order to survive in an undertaking. The free market price is the surest guide to what to produce and in what quantity. When credit is only available from those who hope to profit from lending the scarce money available, there is little likelihood of overexpansion of landholdings or overcapitalization. Not so long as these are dependent on credit. And the farmers who are in desperate straits today are those being crushed by a mountain of debt.

3

Favors for Farmers

by John Chamberlain

There is not room in this selection of articles to include in full the outstanding analysis of The Great Farm Problem *by William H. Peterson (Regnery, 1959). But it is appropriate to include the review of that book by John Chamberlain, chief reviewer for* The Freeman *since 1956 when it became the outlet for materials from The Foundation for Economic Education. As a long-time journalist, reviewer, editor, and analyst of current economic and political affairs, John Chamberlain well deserves a hearing on the farm problem.*

T he farmer in America has always been a member of a favored class. He was favored in the beginning by nature: there was free land in the colonies virtually for the taking. He was favored in Jeffersonian times by the simple fact that he constituted a majority (a century ago our population was 80 per cent rural, and it took one farmer to feed himself and three others). The political bias in favor of the farmer was written into the Constitution itself, with its provision for two senators—no more, no less—from each state regardless of population densities. With the Constitution as his shield and buckler, the farmer—by way of Farm Bloc "logrolling" trades with the industrial states—has always had his political way.

He has, of course, had to reckon with the shade of Alexander Hamilton, who went "one up" on Thomas Jefferson and his agrarian supporters by putting over the idea that industry deserved its subsidy in the form of the protective tariff. I blush to recall that I once cited the tariff as a justification for the counter-subsidizing of the farmer through the Agricultural Adjustment Administration. Superficially considered, it seemed plausible to assert that one good bit of graft deserved another.

But, in retrospect, one wonders just how much the farmer actually suffered from the tariff. The argument used to be that he sold his crops at free world market prices and then had the devil's own time trying to stretch his income so that he might meet the protected prices of industry. What he spent his big sums of money on, however, was machinery—and our mass production machine-making industry (cars, tractors, and so on) has never been particularly favored by the protectionists. As for the farmer's food and housing, they ordinarily came cheap—far cheaper, indeed, than the city man's food and rent. Besides, in the period after the Civil War, the farmer could get a quarter section of land in the West merely by complying with the easy terms of the Homestead Act. Railroads, of course, got a comparable land subsidy—but other industries had to pay for their real estate.

Special Treatment Forever?

Since the American farmer, historically, has been a very decent member of society, no one begrudges him his original free land. But does the fact that he was originally favored by the emptiness of the North American continent give him a claim to special treatment forever? In his *The Great Farm Problem* (Regnery, 235 pages), William H. Peterson, associate professor of economics at New York University, says "no." Farming may be a way of life, but it is a way that loses all its historic virtues of independence and democratic free-masonry once it is made the object of a "charity" that is not forthcoming in proportionate amounts to other ways of life. Blacksmithing and carriage making were once "ways of life," too—but the village smith of Longfellow's poem never was sufficiently numerous to get a pressure group going for him in the U.S. Senate, so he had to transform himself into a diemaker or an automobile mechanic to live. The farmer, on the other hand, has been able to get his fabled "independence" underwritten at the automobile mechanic's expense—and in getting something for nothing he has become hypocritical.

Professor Peterson goes deep into the colonial origins of agrarianism. The historical sections of his book present a succinct recital of the problems, mainly revolving around the currency question, of a century and a half of political agitation. Classically, the West and South wanted cheap money—whether in the form of greenbacks or the free coinage of silver at a sixteen-to-one ratio to gold. The argument was that it was not Christian to squeeze a debtor to favor an abstraction such as "Wall Street." But this was to assume that the creditor had originally made his money in some easy, not quite legitimate way, and that he "owed" it to society to lose it. In any case, the stereotype of the virtuous debtor and the wicked "Wall Street" moneylender has been called into question by recent scholarship.

It turns out on investigation that big eastern bankers lent very little to western farmers: as Allan G. Bogue has shown in his *Money at Interest* (Cornell University Press), it was more often the small mortgage company, often situated in the Mississippi Valley, which helped the farmer get cash when he needed it.

Since it took only about a thousand dollars in cash plus a government grant in land to get a Nebraska farmer and his family started in life in the 1880s, it is hard to justify the argument that "bankers" were the root cause of the Populist and Bryanite agrarian "crusades." It was nature—in the form of the drought cycle—that was to blame. And it would have taken more than greenbacks or free silver to save the farmer who had moved too far out on the high plains from the consequences of his mistaken judgment about climate.

Wartime Land Boom

Professor Peterson makes it indubitably plain that the twentieth century farmer got into trouble when he was caught up in World War I hysteria. During the years when the European farmer's acres were being trampled by armies, the international price of American foodstuffs naturally rocketed. Anyone with half an eye could have foreseen that the high prices were destined to be short-lived. Yet farmers went greedily into long-term debt to take advantage of what was bound to be a short-term advantage. Naturally, they were stuck with their mortgages when peace brought an end to $3.40 wheat and $2.00 corn. Moreover, many of the mortgages had been taken out on submarginal land which could hardly support even debt-free production in times of world plenty.

Since the farmer had always been pampered politically, he thought it incumbent on the rest of the population to bail him out for his unfortunate World War I gamble. Accordingly, scheme after scheme was offered in Congress to give the farmer the benefit of such things as the McNary-Haugen "two-price system." To his credit, Calvin Coolidge vetoed the McNary-Haugen scheme for subsidizing farm exports on two separate occasions. "It cannot be sound," he said, "for all of the people to hire some of the people to produce a crop which neither the producers nor the rest of the people want." The Republicans later gave way to the idea of price-propping and created the Farm Board. And when the New Deal came into office,"farm laws," as Professor Peterson says, "came fast."

The Failure of "Planning"

The real dynamite of Professor Peterson's book is packed into the final chapter, "Analysis," which takes up fully a third of the author's space. What Professor Peterson proves, essentially, is that any and all attempts by the government to solve the farm problem by intervention must end by defeating the intentions of the "planners." Ever since 1933 the individual farmer has always been able to outwit the planner. Money paid to farmers for limiting their planting has been spent on fertilizers and tools that have resulted in bigger surpluses from fewer acres. Land taken out of corn has been put into other crops that have also proved to be redundant. The point has been reached (1959) where every family in the United States is taxed $100 a year (on the average) in order to pay farmers a total of $6 billion a year for withheld production. Yet the surpluses have increased in spite of such gimmicks as the Soil Bank. Dumped abroad or stuck away in caves and warehouses to decay, the surpluses have not resulted in lower prices to the American city consumer. This consumer pays his taxes to give farmers in the United States an average annual subsidy of $1,300 per farm. And then the consumer pays twice over in higher food prices as the government takes the still ever-mounting food surpluses off the local market by such devices as "nonrecourse" loans.

Welfare for the Wealthy

The irony of the whole performance is that most of the subsidy money has gone to the richer farmers, the productive two million who do not need help to sustain them in their "way of life." The remaining two-and-one-half million farmers who might argue that they need a subsidy to stay on the land actually get very little money from the government. (Professor Peterson's figures show that the small farmer, with less than $2,500 market sales a year, gets a mere $109 in price support and stabilization costs where the big farmer with sales of $5,000 or more gets $1,993.) In consequence of the disparity in supports, the small farmer has been giving up his "way of life." Despite all the crocodile tears shed by the farm interventionists, there has been a drop of 28 per cent in total farm workers since the beginning of World War II. In 1940 there were 1,600,000 cotton farmers; today there are only 850,000. The farmers who have been pushed out into city life are not needed on the farm, for in the past two decades the remaining farmers have increased total U. S. agricultural production by some 35 per cent. By the same token, however, the remaining farmers are not the ones for whom the interventionist theorists used to weep.

Professor Peterson, following Henry Hazlitt, has a solution for the "great farm problem." He would cut subsidies to nothing within a given period of time. This would bring supply and demand—and future plantings—into a natural balance; and the good farmer would find himself a free man once more. As for the uneconomic farmer, he must accommodate himself to the fact of change. It is not a happy circumstance to give up a cherished "way of life," but his sons are quitting the farm anyway. It is best for him and for the nation to face reality.

4

Farm Policy—Now What?

by William H. Peterson

As suggested in the introduction of the previous chapter, Dr. William H. Peterson's interest in The Great Farm Problem *was fully expressed in the 1959 volume of that title. He currently is the director of the Center for Economic Education and the Scott L. Probasco Jr. Professor of Free Enterprise at the University of Tennessee at Chattanooga.*

This article from the July 1983 Freeman *updates many of the references to farm population, production, and other statistical measures mentioned in some of the earlier essays included in this section.*

President Reagan proclaims his new payments-in-kind (PIK) program to give farmers surplus grain plus cash if they cut production substantially in the next two years as "highly innovative." Is it really? FDR had a similar program for cotton farmers, and President Kennedy had much the same scheme for feed-grain producers. Neither the Roosevelt nor Kennedy plan proved effective.

Indeed, more than a half-century of aggressive farm intervention costing hundreds of billions of dollars in subsidies spells out a record of unremitting failure and frustration, with the farmers themselves the ultimate losers.

In 1929, for example, President Hoover set up the Federal Farm Board to stabilize crop prices. By the end of his administration the Board had gone through more than $300 million of its $500 million in operating capital, with nothing to show for it but record farm foreclosures. Every time the Board had a modicum of success, production would shoot up, foreign markets would fade away, and heavy inventories would overhang the market like the sword of Damocles. Soon President Hoover recommended the next logical step of price intervention: production restrictions—withdrawing land from cultivation, slaughtering young animals, plowing under crops. President Roosevelt and his successors put these and other restrictions into practice.

Thus the pattern for some five decades of farm intervention was set: production incentives such as price supports and crop insurance, on the one hand, and production curbs such as acreage allotments and marketing quotas, on the other. Generally the production incentives have won, burdening the government and taxpayer with huge stockpiles of food and fiber over the years. The stockpiles, in turn, have forced the government into such welfare ventures as food stamps, school lunches, senior citizen "nutritional programs," "Food for Peace" foreign giveaways, and so on.

The rub with modern farm policy, then, is its useless and quite irrational attempt to repeal the law of supply and demand—to reinvent the wheel. The unhampered price mechanism, in other words, ever pulls supply and demand toward equilibrium, leading to optimum efficiency and economic growth and assuring that whenever shortages or surpluses do emerge they are fleeting and short-lived.

The further rub is that *the farmer to be saved wasn't.* Ultimately he was burned and he, like his forebears, quit the farm for other pursuits, causing a massive change in the composition of the American population. The *1981 Statistical Abstract of the U.S.* tells the story:

	Farm population (millions)	Per cent of total population
1930	30.5	24.9
1940	30.5	23.2
1950	23.0	15.3
1960	15.6	8.7
1970	9.7	4.8
1980	7.2	3.3

In a like way, American agriculture, notwithstanding the lure of subsidies, offers fewer and fewer job opportunities as farmer-entrepreneurs have automated their production. Note how the number of full-time farm jobs, including those of farm operators, their family members doing farm work, and hired hands has plummeted over a 50-year span.

But as the number of farms and farm employment has dropped in this period the size of farms has nearly tripled in entrepreneurial response to the economies of scale over the years.

Moreover, despite all manner of government controls, farm productivity has generally raced ahead of nonfarm productivity in recent decades. From the 1950–1954 period to the 1975–1979 period, for example, the annual average

	Farm employment (millions)	Per cent civilian labor force
1930	12.5	25.8
1940	11.0	19.8
1950	9.9	15.9
1960	7.1	10.2
1970	4.5	5.4
1980	3.7	3.5

yield of corn leaped from 39.4 to 95.2 bushels per acre, wheat from 17.3 to 31.4 bushels per acre, potatoes from 15,100 to 26,200 pounds per acre, milk from 5,400 to 11,000 pounds per cow, and eggs from 181 to 236 per laying chicken.

In the same periods, annual average manhours necessary to produce each 100 pounds of chicken broilers dropped from 2.4 to .1, reflecting enormous acceleration in automated broiler production and a reduction in manhour requirements by 96 per cent in a 25-year stretch. During this same period, turkey production automation was not quite so rapid. Here, 6.8 manhours were required to produce each 100 pounds of turkeys, on an annual average basis, in the 1950–1954 period, against only .5 manhours in the 1975–1979 period, thereby reflecting a 93 per cent manhour reduction in turkey production.

About the only winners I can find in America's farm picture are the farm politician and the farm bureaucrat. The bureaucrat really farms the farmer. While the number of farms and the farm population have plummeted, the number of

	Farms (millions)	Average farm size (acres)
1930	6.5	151
1940	6.3	167
1950	5.6	213
1960	4.0	297
1970	2.9	374
1980	2.4	429

employees at the Agriculture Department has grown like weeds. In 1930 there were 26,050 employees, 98,694 in 1960, and 129,139 in 1980.

Clearly depopulation of the farm sector has weakened the farm bloc but only relatively. Last November (1982) all 21 Democratic members of the House Agriculture Committee seeking re-election held on to their seats while the GOP saw 5 of their 19 members defeated, including ranking member William D. Wampler of Virginia and second-ranking Paul Findley of Illinois, a key Administration supporter on farm bills. So regardless of the irrationality and colossal waste of modern farm policy, the immediate outlook is for more of the same.

But the longer-run outlook seems saner. As farms more and more come into stronger hands and grow in size, farmers will tend to demand more of a no-nonsense farm policy. Then increasingly unhampered farm entrepreneurship can play a more constructive role for the farmer, the consumer, and the economy. For today's farmer, after all, is still a private property-holding, technologically astute, business entrepreneur. And when he becomes numerically smaller still and hence no longer fair game for politicians and bureaucrats, when, in other words, he becomes just another unsubsidized businessman (if in dungarees), he will thrive.

5

Why the President Said No

by Grover Cleveland

No, that was not President Cleveland's title for his veto message. But it is the title under which these passages have been reprinted a number of times in The Freeman *and other Foundation releases.*

The President in 1887 understood and sought to explain to Congress and the American people why it would lead to grave problems if Government tried to support the people. That, it might be said, was one of the earlier outcroppings and a warning against the farm problem.

I return without my approval House Bill No. 10203, entitled "An act to enable the Commissioner of Agriculture to make a special distribution of seeds in the drought-stricken counties of Texas, and making an appropriation [of $10,000] therefor."

It is represented that a long-continued and extensive drought has existed in certain portions of the State of Texas, resulting in a failure of crops and consequent distress and destitution.

Though there has been some difference in statements concerning the extent of the people's needs in the localities thus affected, there seems to be no doubt that there has existed a condition calling for relief; and I am willing to believe that, notwithstanding the aid already furnished, a donation of seed grain to the farmers located in this region, to enable them to put in new crops, would serve to avert a continuance or return of an unfortunate blight.

And yet I feel obliged to withhold my approval of the plan, as proposed by this bill, to indulge a benevolent and charitable sentiment through the appropriation of public funds for that purpose.

I can find no warrant for such an appropriation in the Constitution, and I do not believe that the power and duty of the General Government ought to be extended to the relief of individual suffering which is in no manner properly related to the public service or benefit. A prevalent tendency to disregard the limited mission of this power and duty should, I think, be steadfastly resisted, to the end that the lesson should be constantly enforced that *though the people support the Government the Government should not support the people.* [Emphasis added.]

The friendliness and charity of our countrymen can always be relied upon to relieve their fellow-citizens in misfortune. This has been repeatedly and quite lately demonstrated. Federal aid in such cases encourages the expectation of paternal care on the part of the Government and weakens the sturdiness of our national character, while it prevents the indulgence among our people of that kindly sentiment and conduct which strengthens the bonds of a common brotherhood.

Part Two

The Domestic Impact of Farm Policies

I n viewing the farm problem in perspective, as done in the first part of this
volume, it begins to be clear that the problem is not so much the creation
of farmers as it is a matter of policy. National policy, that is, and that
means political regulation and control.

So it is time to review those policies from at least two major standpoints: (1)
The domestic impact and (2) International implications. In this Part Two are
included essays on the nature and effect of price supports in general, with
emphasis on farm price supports. What such price intervention amounts to is a
closure of the market and subjection of a great industry, the farming industry, to
the inherent handicaps of socialism. One aspect of the farm problem often
overlooked has to do with food stamps and distribution of surplus commodities
to the needy. Finally, there are the anomalies and contradictions, the indirect
consequences of good intentions, the continuing plight of agriculture today after
so much ''help.''

6

Price Supports

by W.M. Curtiss

Dr. W.M. Curtiss came from a farm in Illinois to do graduate work in agricultural economics at Cornell. A part of that training included a year in China as assistant to J. Lossing Buck (husband of Pearl Buck) concerned with economic and sociological aspects of Chinese agriculture. Dr. Curtiss joined the staff of FEE in 1946, serving in many ways. One of his earlier studies published in 1949 was this essay on "Price Supports," pointing out how such intervention disrupts the market guidance of production and consumption and leads producers and consumers into disastrous errors of over-expansion, inefficiency, and chaos.

Stripped to its essentials, the basic objective of the over-all price support program for agriculture is to prevent a general collapse in farm prices such as occurred in 1921 and 1929. Few persons disagree with the desirability of the objective; the basic disagreement lies in whether or not price supports are a suitable means to this end.

Prices of goods and services may be compared with water in a lake. Ripples and waves on the surface of the lake correspond to the prices of individual commodities. They rise and fall in varying degrees depending on supply and demand conditions for each commodity, even though the over-all level of the lake may not change. The level of the lake itself rises and falls because of what happens at the inlet and outlet of the lake. A price support or ceiling on one commodity may change the height of that particular ripple, but it is offset by the height of others. It has little or no effect on the over-all level of the lake, the general price level.

Changes in the prices of individual commodities, constantly going on even in a stable economy, serve a useful and important function. We saw this function in operation in the fall of 1948 in the relation of the price of hogs to corn. With a very short corn crop in 1947, corn prices advanced relative to hogs. And farmers economized in the feeding of corn. In 1948, with a very large corn crop, farmers received the signal—cheaper corn—to expand the feeding of corn to hogs and other livestock. These adjustments run all through our economy. In a free market, farmers will constantly shift their production of cabbage, sweet corn and all other crops and livestock products to meet changing demand and supply conditions. When the signals are tampered with, faulty prices may call for too little of this or too much of that so that consumers are unable to satisfy their demands in the market.

It is not denied that the legal price of a single commodity can be maintained above or below where it would be in a free market. The price of potatoes, for example, could be set at 25 cents a bushel or at $25 a bushel and if a large enough number of policemen were assigned to the job of rationing the very small production at 25 cents, or of restricting the very great attempted production at $25, the price might be maintained. But even if this were done for one commodity, or for many commodities, the major problem of preventing general inflation or deflation would not be solved.

The solution of the problem of the giant swings in the general price level lies in the area of the monetary and fiscal policy of the nation and is outside the scope of this discussion.

It might be asserted that price supports or price ceilings on individual commodities are not effective in preventing major inflationary and deflationary swings, and end the discussion here. But it is important to point out some of the harmful effects of such programs.

Price supports are a one-sided form of price control. Price control is a part of the more important question, namely, whether the nation shall have an economy of free markets, or whether it shall be one of price control leading to production control, allocation of labor, and ultimately, socialism. It matters little whether the outcome of the latter choice is called Democratic Socialism, Socialized Capitalism, State Socialism, Social Democracy, Marxian Socialism, Collectivism or just plain Communism.

The Function of the Free Price Mechanism

A free market system is perhaps the most essential ingredient of a voluntary economy. Without this freedom to express his wants—and thus to have a hand in guiding production and consumption—man can hardly be called free.

The sole purpose of economic production is to cater to the wants of consumers and thus to satisfy the wants of both producers and consumers. The most satisfactory method by which consumers can make their preferences known to producers—and thus to guide production—is through the free price system. Millions of consumers are thereby enabled to vote for or against individual products by their acceptance (purchase) or rejection of items of consumption.

Another method of guiding production and consumption is to have the decision of a single individual or of a central bureau substituted for the decisions of millions of individuals interested in that particular or related commodity. There is no third choice. Either the free price system will be permitted to do the job or it will not. The only way in which there is a middle ground is in the sense that not all items of goods and services may be under control. Some may be free while others are controlled. But there is abundant evidence to indicate that, once started, price control spreads because of the complex influence which products have on each other. First, the price of a single item may be controlled. Then it is found desirable to control its substitute and then the substitutes for the substitute, and so on.

It must be assumed that those who favor price control of a commodity— whether it be price supports, price ceilings, subsidies, marketing agreements, forward pricing or other forms—believe that the price should be either higher or lower than it would be if voluntarily arrived at by a willing buyer and a willing seller. Otherwise it would not be price control.

A Delicate Instrument

The free price mechanism is as delicate as a fine precision instrument with millions of moving parts. Each part contributes to the operation of the whole. It operates so smoothly that it is sometimes called automatic. But it is anything but automatic in the sense that it runs without direction.

Consider, for example, some of the factors which, together, make the price of a bushel of wheat. They include the prospects for rain in the wheat country, the amount of snow in the mountains, the amount of insect damage, the availability of harvest help and machinery, the burning of a few thousand bushels in a local elevator, the availability of boxcars for shipping, the amount of wheat fed to livestock, the production of wheat in Canada, China and Russia, and literally thousands of other things that are wrapped up in what we call supply, or prospective supply.

The price of wheat is influenced by the price of oats, corn, potatoes, rye and many other competing crops. The amount of money in the country and the freeness of persons' spending of it, the amount of wheat purchased for foreign account, the price of automobiles and radios, and an unknown number of other factors all have a bearing.

No one person or bureau can possibly know all the contributing reasons why I reject a radio offered at $12.98 and you decide to buy it. Perhaps my wife wants a new hat and yours doesn't. Fortunately it is not necessary that each buyer and seller have all this information. All that is necessary to consummate a sale is for a seller to say, "I am willing to sell," and the buyer to say, "I am willing to buy" at the same price. The seller may say, "I can't continue to sell for that and stay in business," or the buyer may say, "I can't continue to pay that much and stay in business." Suffice it to say, the exchange was made. And in view of the alternatives known to each party, the exchange was agreeable to both. A price set arbitrarily at a point different from where a willing buyer and seller would voluntarily set it, is certain to make one of the parties feel he was cheated. In fact, it does cheat one of them.

Who Should Plan?

The basic question involved here is not whether there should be economic planning, but rather who should do it. Economic planning there will be. It will be done either by millions of individuals who are directly concerned, each making his own independent decisions, or it will be done by a central planning committee, given power to ignore the judgment of these individuals.

A central statistical bureau may assemble volumes of data concerning the demand for and supply of a certain commodity. There is a strong temptation for the bureau then to feel that it knows so much more about conditions than a single producer or consumer can possibly know, that it can therefore decide the price more wisely. Actually, they cannot have all the pertinent facts and certainly not the most important ones which individuals use in deciding on whether or not to buy a certain item.

The delicate free price mechanism works miracles in guiding workers into each branch of the economy and in guiding the use of raw materials and other resources according to the wishes of consumers. Some have argued that our economy has become too complex to let it run without central planning. Actually, the more complex it becomes, the more important it is to have the economic planning done by the individuals concerned; the more important it becomes to have their decisions reported in a free market.

The free market serves as a guide to persons in deciding whether they should be dentists, doctors, farmers, lawyers, school teachers, grocery clerks or bank clerks. When this function of price is tampered with, it becomes necessary to dictate to the workers what jobs they shall fill and how and where they shall fill them. England has already discovered this.

The free price system is a guide as to how much steel shall be used for tractors, for automobiles, for housing, for toys, for railroads and for other purposes. It suggests whether oil or gas or coal shall be used for heating a house. It serves as a guide in determining how much feed grain shall be fed to dairy cows, or hens, or hogs. This system tells the users of a commodity whether to economize in its use or to expand it. It tells the potato producer, for example, how many acres to plant and whether to harvest all of his crop or leave the smaller potatoes on the ground at harvest time. It suggests how much fertilizer to use and whether or not it will pay him to put in an irrigation system. It tells him whether he will profit more by packing his crop in wholesale lots or in consumer packages. All this guidance appears almost accidental and without direction, but behind it all is a vast amount of experience, study and thought by all of the persons concerned. The result is that the crop moves to market in an extremely orderly fashion just meeting the demand. All this serves to guide producers of next year's crop.

Costs of Central Planning

It is not denied that a central planning bureau *could* make decisions (disregarding the quality of these decisions) involving the jobs which each person should fill, as well as the amount of production and the distribution of each individual commodity. This, of course, is the design of a planned economy. Space will not permit a complete discussion of the cost of a planned economy. This cost involves the tremendous staff of planners, administrators and policemen who might be otherwise employed in the production and distribution of goods and services. It involves the question of the right of an individual to the product of his own labor; it involves the question of incentives to high production which come with this right. It involves the satisfactions which individuals gain from making decisions in questions involving themselves. In short, the whole question of human liberty and the purpose of life itself is tied up in this one issue.

If the price of a commodity is arbitrarily set by a central bureau, it might conceivably be where it would have been in a free market at some place and at one time. If so, it serves no purpose at that time and place. It is likely to be wrong at all other places and at all other times because no central bureau can possibly master all of the differentials that a free market solves.

There is no one price for a commodity like potatoes. There are literally thousands of different prices, depending on different conditions, making up what we think of as "the market price." And strangely enough, in a free market, each of the many different prices is the "right" price for the given situation.

Price is somewhat like the signal which the captain on the bridge of a ship sends to the engine room or the instructions he gives to the helmsman. If the signal is right, the ship stays on its course. If it is wrong, the ship cannot go where it is intended it should go. Price is a signal to both producers and consumers of a commodity as well as to all of the agencies involved in distribution. We have had experience with mixing up the signals. We have seen potato prices set too low with a resulting potato famine before a new crop came along. Under the fixed low prices, the signal to economize in the use of potatoes failed to reach consumers. Had this faulty signal continued, it would also have been interpreted by producers to cut future production. A similar situation has existed in the rents of dwellings which were fixed too low. The signal to renters was not to economize on space but to expand. And they did just that. The signal to build new housing was not given. The result was that we had a housing "famine."

Tampering with the Signal

When the price of a commodity is set lower by controls than the market would set it, the product becomes scarce and its allocation becomes a problem. When a free price is prohibited from rationing a product, some other method must be used. It may be done outside the law in black markets, or with tickets, or special favoritism, or by some other method.

In the other direction, we have had experience with arbitrarily setting the prices of a commodity higher than a free market would set them. Price supports contemplate doing this. In such a situation, a wrong signal is sent to both producers and consumers, with the result that a "surplus" arises. The consumer does not buy the whole supply, because the price is higher than he will pay for the amount offered. The producer is encouraged to expand the production of a commodity already in unsalable supply.

A system of price supports where prices are maintained above the free market level by government is not unlike a system tried by a number of agricultural marketing cooperatives years ago. They found that by keeping prices too high, they were encouraging more and more production and discouraging consumption. They discovered they were building up a larger and larger carry-over from one crop to the next. One after another, cooperatives based on this principle either failed, or changed their policy. An important difference, of course, between the government and a private cooperative following such a policy is that the government can use its taxing power to make up losses and can conceal the error for a longer time by sending the bill for "services rendered" to others.

Whereas "scarcities," due to setting prices too low, require some kind of a rationing system, "surpluses," due to setting prices too high, require some kind of a disposal plan as well as arbitrary production controls. Otherwise, farmers are paid from taxes to expand acreage or to put in irrigation systems, or to use heavy applications for fertilizer to produce potatoes to be used for livestock feed or to be destroyed.

Subsidize: Control

Agricultural leaders, like leaders in other industries, have long been trying to devise some system to raise the price of their products above free market prices, without at the same time exercising some direct control over production. Such a search seems doomed to failure because of the very nature of the price system. If prices of individual commodities are too high, they stimulate too much production and too little consumption at that level of prices; some kinds of production controls thus become necessary unless the government dumps its surplus abroad or gives it away or diverts it into other uses at home. If prices are too low, some other type of stimulus such as subsidies or direct compulsion is required to bring out the production assumed necessary. It is but a short step from there to the British system where prices are guaranteed and producers told what to produce. It is a still shorter step from that to complete nationalization of the industry. Our own Supreme Court has stated that government may properly regulate that which it subsidizes.

Another consequence of a price support which holds a price above where it would be in a free market is its effect in keeping less efficient producers in business. A competitive economy, based on free market prices, has been an important factor in improving efficiency in all types of business. The market price serves as a signal to the high cost or less efficient producer to use his talents and resources elsewhere. Think what would be the situation in the automobile business today if, through support prices, all the hundreds of auto manufacturers that have fallen by the wayside had been kept in business at public expense. Suppose we had adopted a system of price supports to keep buggy manufacturers in business.

Planning Dilemma

Instead of a free market for potatoes, suppose the price is arbitrarily set above the market. What happens? Not only are the less efficient producers encouraged to stay in the potato business, but also new producers who are still less efficient may be drawn in. As a result, more potatoes may be produced than can be sold at the designated price. The problem of the planners now is what to do about the surplus production. They may decide that acreage should be reduced or marketing quotas should be established. How will they do it? Your guess is as good as mine because it is now a political football. They may decide to scale down each grower's acreage by the same percentage. It would be virtually impossible to set up a workable formula that would affect nearby areas and areas far from the market, the way a free price would. The method chosen is not likely to be one that will eliminate the less efficient producers.

This illustrates some of the problems involved on the production side when free markets are interfered with. Problems on the consumption side are just as involved and critical. Consumers are prevented from having a hand in directing production according to their wishes. It is self-evident that people can consume no more than what is produced. The free market permits consumers to express a choice for fewer potatoes at a higher price per bushel together with the thing produced by those who were formerly potato producers. It permits them to make this choice if they wish, in preference to having more and cheaper potatoes, but without the production of the other things. Certainly, few consumers would voluntarily call for so bountiful a supply of potatoes that they be fed to livestock, used for fertilizer or be destroyed.

Over the years, less efficient farmers have found that they could not meet the competition of more efficient ones. In our expanding economy they have found their services useful elsewhere. This has made it possible for the efficiency of our farms to increase from the point where an average farm produced little more than enough for the farmer and his family to where a farm family now feeds itself and a good many other families. The farmer not only feeds his family better but also gains from the production of automobiles, refrigerators, bathtubs, transportation, entertainment, education, churches, and many, many other goods and services produced by non-farmers.

Competition And Progress

This kind of progress will continue only with competition and free markets. It is conceivable that farm efficiency can further develop to a point where only one family in twenty or thirty will be required to raise the nation's food supply. Such progress cannot continue if inefficient production is encouraged.

Efficient farm producers have nothing to fear from competition. It is the lack of competition that they should fear. It has been estimated that one-third of the farmers produce 80 per cent of the nation's food. Price supports will tend to keep in competition the least efficient one-third of the farmers who produce only 4 per cent of the food and who might far better be doing something else.

Another aspect of price supports for agricultural products is the matter of special privileges for minority groups. Under a political system such as ours, there is a tendency for certain groups to seek special privileges at the expense of other groups. If they are strong enough politically, they may be able to obtain them. Agriculture has been and still may be strong politically. But it is rapidly becoming a smaller and smaller minority. In the interest of equal rights for all, it would seem that farmers would gain more in the long run by promoting the idea of no special privilege for any group.

An argument frequently used by agricultural leaders for various farm programs is that labor and other types of business have "enjoyed" advantages in the form of tariffs and other devices, and that therefore agriculture is entitled to a share of "protection." These are exactly the tactics used in a pressure-group economy. Two wrongs do not make a right. And in the end, this process leads to a thoroughly confused situation where vast numbers of persons become willing to turn the whole sorry mess over to government, as they are rapidly doing in England and have done in other nations of the world.

Summarizing briefly, price supports, like other forms of price control, are not an answer to the important problem of bringing reasonable stability to our economy—of eliminating major swings in our general price level caused by monetary inflation and deflation. In addition to their failure to reach this objective, price supports rob us of the most important function of free prices— the guiding of production and consumption of goods and services in accordance with the wishes of those directly concerned.

Finally—and this is most important—price controls must be accompanied by controls of production and consumption. It cannot be otherwise. Such controls lead to complete economic domination of citizens by agents of the State.

7

Market Closed

by Paul L. Poirot

Paul Poirot was managing editor of The Freeman *for many years. This essay from the July 1971 issue was inspired by questions from a friend, a farmer in New York, who was concerned about a pending marketing order that would be applicable to his activities and products. This was an attempt to show how such orders establish a monopoly or cartel arrangement, thereby closing off that special branch of an industry from the beneficent forces of market pricing and guidance.*

T his little piggy went to market. But the market was closed—indefinitely—by order of the government.

There had been a lot of complaints about the market:

- It takes a person at his word and holds him responsible for his actions.
- It allows unwanted resources to go unclaimed and unused.
- It permits scarce and valuable resources to be owned and controlled by the highest bidder.
- It allows foreigners to compete on equal terms with domestic suppliers and buyers.
- It lets prices for goods and services rise or fall in response to demand and supply.
- It permits people to hire or to work for one another on terms mutually agreeable.
- It lets buyers and sellers use anything they please as money.
- It lets the owner consume, save, offer for sale, or otherwise use, waste, pollute, or abuse his property as he chooses.
- It allows a person to succeed or fail in accordance with his decisions and actions.
- It allows a person to specialize in any business or profession, or to live a life of self-subsistence, as he chooses.

● It allows people to congregate in centers of trade and culture.

In short, the market respects the dignity of every human being and lets him do just as he pleases with what is properly his own, leaving him free to reap the benefits and suffer the consequences of his own actions.

A market economy can hardly be described as a natural development, such as might be found among plants, bees, birds, or animals in the wild. It is the result, rather, of human reason applied to the problems of the individual in society. The theory or premise behind the market is that the most practicable and desirable form of society is one that maximizes personal freedom of choice and minimizes violence among men. Insofar as possible, let man do as he pleases, acting alone or in strictly voluntary association with others. And this is the purpose of the market: to facilitate voluntary association and trade.

However, by definition and by nature, a voluntary association is unable to police itself, has no means of enforcing the rules of the association within its own membership and no means of protecting itself from nonmembers. The market, for instance, has no market method of coping with a buyer or a seller who resorts to coercion or fraud to effect a trade, no way to keep the market open and operating in the face of those who would close it by violent methods.

So, the human reason that calls for a market economy, in order to maximize the exercise of personal freedom of choice, also demands a framework of government, a government strictly limited in scope and function to policing the market, protecting the life and property of everyone who comes to trade in peace, and making sure that no person or group is permitted to block any peaceful trader from the market. This appears to be the minimum governmental force required to police the market and thus maximize the freedom of the individual, release his creative energies for peaceful production and trade, reduce his incentive and temptation to resort to violence to obtain or defend what he wants.

In other words, the optimum release of creative human energy requires a framework—or perhaps a leavening—of organized police power, a government of strictly limited scope and purpose to minimize violence among men. If this reasoning be correct, it suggests a corollary proposition: *Any expansion or extension of governmental force beyond the minimum required to police the market necessarily and inevitably drives individuals and groups to acts of violence against one another.* Such aggravated violence involves destruction of human and other resources that might otherwise have been turned to peaceful and constructive use.

The Ultimate Intervention

Such was the situation on the fateful day our hypothetical "little piggy" went to market and found it closed. Not satisfied with the risks and pressures of open competition, this and that person and group had sought and obtained government intervention in its own behalf:

- protection against foreign suppliers of goods and services.
- a special license or exclusive trading privilege.
- a right to strike and keep competitors from taking the job vacated.
- zoning ordinances to force neighbors to keep their distance.
- unlimited supplies of money and credit.
- fair trade laws to prevent price cutting.
- minimum wage laws.
- laws to hold prices up, or to hold prices down.
- rent control laws.
- low-cost public housing projects.
- guaranteed income in old age, or at any age.
- free schooling, medical care, dental care, legal aid, food stamps.
- a little privilege here, and a little pressure there, and so forth and so on.

Yet, the more the government is asked to intervene on behalf of some persons and groups at the expense of others, the more difficult it is for anyone to compete in the open market to serve himself by peacefully serving others. No sooner is a special privilege granted by government to a particular person or group than other persons or groups begin fighting to obtain "their fair share." And whatever the grant of privilege or power, it is never enough; the beneficiaries demand more, and turn to violence to get it.

From Violence to Famine

The market cannot cope with violence, which destroys savings and investments, tools and facilities of production, the incentive to specialize and trade. This coercive detour of the market leads back toward conditions of famine and starvation chronically suffered by slaves, serfs, and socialists. People unfree or unwilling to compete in the market for possession and use of scarce resources inevitably find themselves trying to subsist on rations. Instead of faring each according to his ability and his effort, each hopes to share according to his need. The individual ceases to be responsible for what he produces or consumes; these choices are made for him by someone else. He stands to gain or lose nothing by producing more or less. Nor is it to his advantage to save, since his savings would be confiscated. The share rationed to him is in proportion to his lack of productivity. When violence closes the market, famine cannot be far behind.

One need not rely on theory or imagination to test the procedures and effects of closing the market. In the *Communist Manifesto* of 1848, Karl Marx drew up the blueprint, spelled out various of the most important measures "to centralize all instruments of production in the hands of the state." The blueprint has been followed, the measures applied, in Russia, China, Cuba, and other lands. The markets have been closed, displaced by coercive collectivism. And the inevitable consequence in each case has been degrading poverty and famine.

In a sense, and in the light of the trend of developments in the United States in recent decades, Marx seems to have been remarkably prophetic in his list of ten steps toward compulsory collectivism. On the other hand, it should have required no great flash of insight by some genius, even as far back as 1848, to foresee what might be some of the consequences if a system of coercion were to displace the market system of open competition and voluntary exchange.

Experiences in Agriculture

In any event, whether or not Marx realized what he was doing, understood what he was saying, or knew where his ideas were leading in 1848, there would seem to be little excuse for confusion about the results of coercion in the latter part of the twentieth century. Indeed, one need not look beyond quite recent domestic experiments and experiences in agriculture for necessary proof of the failure of coercive practices and the reasons why nothing is to be gained by any person or group through further ventures in that direction.

What, for instance, have the cotton growers of the United States gained for their efforts over the past fifty years to get more for their product than the competitive market would allow? True, they have gotten some subsidy payments from taxpayers, but along with the subsidies have come stringent government regulations and controls and quotas and restraints of one kind and another. The values of quotas and allotments have been built into the price of the land to which they are tied, and that higher priced land carries ever higher taxes. Further, the withholding of American grown cotton from the market has opened the door inadvertently, not only to foreign growers of cotton but more especially to domestic producers of rayon, nylon, and a host of other synthetic fibers. Instead of competing in the open market, American cotton growers are finding themselves more or less bound and gagged on an artificial political pedestal, their own political power dwindling and no bright prospect of a large bloc of satisfied consumers from whom political support might be forthcoming.

Similar, if not identical, experiences could be reported for American growers of wheat, corn, tobacco, rice, peanuts, sugar cane and beets, various fruits, vegetables, nuts, and other specialty crops under marketing orders, agreements, or cartel grants of one kind and another. Nor does the attempted producer-monopoly seem to hold up with greater success when bolstered by international commodity agreements such as those for wheat, cotton, sugar, coffee, and so on. The mathematics of political power simply doesn't work out right to give a relatively small group of specialized producers a great and generous handout from a larger group of frustrated consumers.

A Cauliflower Cartel

Aside from the political impracticality, consider the simple economics of the producer-cartel or monopoly. For the sake of argument or illustration, let's suppose there are 1,000 growers of cauliflower in the United States. Why shouldn't they form an association for the more orderly marketing of high quality cauliflower? In other words, put their heads together and form a monopoly in order to hold supplies from the market and thus obtain higher prices!

Of these thousand growers, one of them is the largest and one the smallest commercial producer of cauliflower in the nation. And there's every likelihood that the larger one achieved his position through efficient production. Chances are that the relatively few of the very large growers are the low-cost, efficient ones, whereas several of the smaller producers may be operating at no profit, perhaps at a loss. (Size, of course, does not necessarily mark success; the point is that some growers are more efficient than others.) Of the thousand growers, no doubt the majority of smaller producers would be very happy to see the few larger ones cut back their output. But why should any large, efficient grower want to thus restrict trade or take himself out of the market? And if he did, what would stop 10,000 other farmers from trying to supply the cauliflower market he had just vacated? Of course, a law would be needed to prohibit cauliflower production by those who could show no previous records of production. And it also would be necessary to prohibit imports of cauliflower from abroad, if the domestic monopoly were to be effective.

So, there would be production and marketing quotas for each of the 1,000 privileged growers, not to mention endless quality controls and other governmental rules and regulations. An efficient cauliflower grower should want no part of any such "protective" arrangement. And if he only knew it, neither should the inefficient loser among the growers wish to be artificially shielded from or blinded to his failure. Far better to know the truth, so that he might turn his labor and other resources immediately to something more potentially profitable to him than cauliflower growing.

Finally, it is not to be supposed that a cauliflower monopoly begins and ends with cauliflower growers. This coercive action affects other persons and groups, some seeking a comparable special privilege for themselves, others seeking opportunities to return to the open market. If all the devious consequences of coercive intervention could be foreseen and understood, it seems unlikely that mature and responsible adults would ever want to try to price themselves out of the market.

Free Market: Who Needs It?

Many people will not be greatly concerned about the producers who may suffer as a consequence of closing the market. Their professed concern is rather for the poor. Who cares about a few producers, some of whom had accumulated sizable fortunes? Why keep the market open for that type of person? Why not try some form of profit-sharing or dividing the wealth or other socialistic program to give the millions of the poor a better chance?

The fact is that the successful businessman or entrepreneur probably would make out pretty well for himself under any system. Whatever "the rules of the game," he'd find his way toward the top. And, sad to say, the poor within a market economy would still be the poor, for the most part, under any other arrangement.

So, it is the poor who stand to lose the most, comparatively, as a consequence of closing the market. The competitive market economy is the only system that channels the creative efforts of the most aggressive and capable individuals into serving the needs and wants of the poor. That is really why we can't afford to let the market be closed.

8

Economic Reality and U.S. Government Farm Programs

by E.C. Pasour, Jr.

This is an analysis and commentary on current front-page news of farm bankruptcies growing out of various programs to help low-income farmers and to stabilize agriculture. It is from The Freeman *of June 1985.*

Dr. Pasour, Professor of Economics at North Carolina State University at Raleigh, concludes that "non-inflationary monetary and fiscal policies plus a more open economy would benefit agriculture far more than the network of costly action programs now in place."

Farm bankruptcies are front-page news. Although the magnitude of the problem has undoubtedly been overstated by the media, there are no hard data on the precise number of farm businesses experiencing financial stress. According to a 1984 survey, less than 20 per cent of all farm operators had debt/asset ratios of 40 per cent or higher.[1] While the USDA on the basis of a recent American Bankers Association survey of agricultural banks found the incidence of farm bankruptcies "relatively low," pleas for government to "do something" are widespread throughout the land.[2]

The paradoxical nature of the call for government action to alleviate the economic distress in U.S. agriculture is too little recognized. As shown in the following analysis, current farm problems are rooted in past government programs.[3] As so often happens when government intervenes, government farm programs not only have failed to achieve their objectives but have created pressures for further intervention to deal with the unforeseen and unintended consequences of these policies.

Despite the fact that U.S. agriculture is often considered to be a bastion of free enterprise, farm programs today are remarkably similar to the protectionist Roosevelt New Deal policies instituted during the Great Depression of the 1930s.

52

Moreover, it is ironic that government outlays for farm programs have increased greatly during the Reagan Administration. The taxpayer cost of farm price support programs alone increased from $4 billion in 1980 to more than $20 billion in 1983—making these programs the most rapidly growing item in the deficit-plagued Federal budget.

Although agriculture escaped the deregulation movement of the late 1970s and early 1980s that affected transportation, banking, and so on, it appears that major changes are likely to occur in U.S. farm policies within the next decade. The pressures for change are due to changing economic conditions and to an increasing public awareness of the effects of past government farm policies.

As the U.S. Congress debates a 1985 farm bill, agricultural policy is at a crossroads with only two choices. The choice is either to continue the existing network of costly programs involving government subsidies and government-sanctioned restrictions on competition that now affect about half the output of U.S. farms or, alternatively, to rely on the competitive market process to bring about appropriate adjustments in production and resource use. In making this choice, it is important to consider the objectives and results of current and past farm programs.

Government Intervention to Assist Low-Income Farmers

Price supports, marketing orders, and other restrictions on competition were instituted to increase farm prices and incomes during the Great Depression when economic conditions in agriculture were greatly different than they are today. While farm incomes, on average, historically have been lower than nonfarm incomes, this is no longer the case. If the half of the farms that are noncommercial rural residences are eliminated from the income statistics, the farm sector has higher family incomes, on average, than the nonfarm sector.[4] Of course, there is no presumption that wages *should* be equal. And, if public policies are instituted to equalize wages in different sectors regardless of underlying economic trends, there is little incentive for labor to adjust in response to changing economic conditions.

Furthermore, government farm programs make the income distribution less equal within agriculture since most farm program benefits are related to farm size. Consequently, when farm product prices are increased by price supports, incomes of small farmers are affected relatively little. Economist William Lesher estimates that just 13 per cent of the farms obtain 45 per cent of direct government payments, while 71 per cent of the farms receive only 22 per cent of the payments.[5] The result is that although farm programs are justified on the basis of helping low-income farmers, it is owners of large farms with incomes quite high relative to nonfarmers who receive most of the benefits.

Government Intervention to "Stabilize Agriculture"

Another goal of farm policy is to "stabilize" farm product prices and income. Despite this often stated goal, there is little doubt that past government policies have contributed to the current financial distress being experienced by substantial numbers of farmers. The record suggests that government attempts to stabilize agricultural markets have been no more successful than similar attempts by government to "fine-tune" the overall level of economic activity during the past 15–20 years. Indeed, much of the current economic distress in U.S. agriculture can be traced directly to inflationary monetary and fiscal policies and to subsidized credit, which induced farmers to overinvest in land and capital facilities during the late 1970s.

Economic instability is often increased by government intervention as Washington political decision makers manipulate agricultural (and other) programs to affect upcoming elections. Prior to the 1976 election, for example, the Ford Administration raised the loan rate on wheat from $1.50 to $2.25 per bushel and tripled the tariff on imported sugar.[6] Similarly, President Carter increased dairy price supports on the eve of the 1980 election. Again, in September 1984 President Reagan changed the rules of the Farmers Home Administration (FmHA) to postpone and reduce farm debt—thereby merely postponing the day of reckoning for many farmers.

The subsidized credit programs operated by the FmHA create an incentive to expand the size of farm operations through borrowing. The high ratio of capital to labor in U.S. agriculture makes farming particularly sensitive to changes in interest rates. When the cost of capital is subsidized, farmers are induced to substitute capital for labor and land. Thus, easy government credit policies undoubtedly have contributed to the recent increase in farm bankruptcies.

The importance of the export market for U.S. farm products increased markedly during the early 1970s. Although the United States is the world's largest exporter of agricultural products, government policies increase uncertainty and instability in export markets. The suspension of grain sales to the Soviet Union in 1980 by President Carter is a prime example. Uncertainty and instability inevitably increase when the demand and price of farm products hinge on unpredictable political factors.

However, it is not only trade restrictions directly affecting agricultural exports that are of importance to U.S. farmers. During the recent recession, the Reagan Administration tightened import restrictions on a range of products including autos, steel, textile products, and motorcycles. Since buyers of U.S. farm products must obtain dollars to make these purchases, such restrictions on imports, whether "voluntary" or involuntary, are especially damaging to U.S.

agriculture. The conclusion is that much of the market instability for U.S. farm products during the past decade can be traced to government policies.

Indirect Effects of Farm Programs

Restrictions on competition inevitably reduce the efficiency of resource use. In current wheat, feed grain, and cotton programs, the government pays U.S. farmers not to till some of the world's most productive farmland. The higher prices for bread, milk, sugar, and other products resulting from price support programs are especially harmful to those with low incomes and create increased pressures for food stamps and other income transfer programs.

There is a cost of production "trap" associated with the operation of all agricultural price support programs. Any effective price support will increase cost of production as increases in product prices are capitalized into prices of land, production rights, and other specialized resources. Thus, if the price of wheat were doubled or tripled to (say) $10 per bushel, prices of land and other specialized resources in wheat production would be bid up so that the expected cost of production, including the return to entrepreneurship, would tend to equal product price.

Since the benefits of farm programs are largely capitalized into higher prices of inputs (especially land), it is the owners of these inputs at that time who benefit. Producers who enter production later receive little benefit from such programs unless price support levels are further increased. Later entrants into production receive higher product prices, but they also have higher costs. Moreover, the increased prices of land and other inputs creates a trap that makes it difficult to abolish farm programs. If price support levels are reduced or abolished, prices of land and other specialized assets decrease—imposing huge losses on current farmers, particularly landowners. The windfall losses would not necessarily be incurred by those who received the gains since many farmers bought land and other farm assets after prices of these assets had already increased and, therefore, did not receive the original windfall.

There is a great deal of public concern about the viability of the small farm. Thus, it is ironic that interest rate subsidies of the FmHA and the CCC (Commodity Credit Corporation) promote the trend toward fewer and larger farms by encouraging the substitution of machinery and other capital inputs for labor. When credit is allocated on the basis of opportunity cost, credit is used by those producers who best accommodate consumer demands. If credit is subsidized, some less productive producers are kept in business, thereby increasing output with lower product prices. Thus, another indirect effect of subsidized credit is to harm those producers *not* receiving preferential treatment in capital markets.

Schizophrenic Nature of Programs

Farm programs are incredibly complex and there is no way to determine the net impact of the network of price supports, marketing orders, credit subsidies, conservation subsidies, food stamps, and other programs financed through the U.S. Department of Agriculture. However, the programs are often inconsistent, having opposite effects on farm product prices. For example, price support programs for milk, sugar, feed grains, wheat, cotton, and tobacco along with food stamp and other subsidized food assistance programs *increase* product prices. On the other hand, government-financed research activities and credit, land, and water subsidies tend to increase output and *decrease* farm product prices.

Expenditures to "stabilize farm prices and income" by reducing output totaled about $20 billion in fiscal 1983. During the same period, expenditures that increase output totaled about $15 billion. If the dollars spent on these programs were equally efficient in achieving their conflicting objectives, some $30 billion may have been spent in 1983 on activities having little (or no) net effect on food costs, farm prices, or farm incomes. That is, because of their opposite effects on product prices, a substantial part of farm program expenditures merely cancel out each other. However, there are important gainers and losers associated with the operation of farm programs as indicated below even if the expenditures, on average, are self-defeating.

The fundamental problem in agriculture, as in other areas, is to achieve the most productive pattern of resource use. There are only two ways of securing economic cooperation—the market system and central direction. There is, in general, a strong case for decentralized competitive markets as the most effective means of coping with constantly changing economic conditions. The competitive entrepreneurial market process is fully as applicable in agriculture as in other economic sectors. The market in agricultural production and marketing activities can do what central planning cannot do: it can utilize the detailed information in millions of minds that cannot be conveyed to any planning authority. In view of the record of past government farm programs, the burden of proof should be on those advocating continuation or expansion of programs that prohibit or inhibit the operation of the entrepreneurial market process.

The value of U.S. farm exports jumped from $8 billion in 1972 to about $44 billion in 1981—a dramatic increase in real terms. The increased dependence of U.S. agriculture on international trade has important implications for domestic agricultural policies since there is a fundamental incompatibility between domestic agricultural price support programs and free international trade. When domestic prices of dairy, tobacco, peanut, sugar, and other products are raised above the world price, imports must be restricted to prevent domestic

consumers from purchasing lower priced imports. As the dependence of U.S. agriculture on exports increases, the liberalization of trade becomes increasingly important. However, the United States cannot be a credible proponent of free trade as long as U.S. farmers operate under an umbrella of protectionist domestic agricultural policies.

Implications and Conclusions

The effect of government-enforced restrictions on competition in agriculture is to increase income to wheat growers, sugar producers, dairy farmers, and other small groups at the expense of the public at large. Consumers and taxpayers bear the major costs of government farm programs. Price support programs mean that consumers face higher prices of milk, sugar, peanuts, tobacco, oranges, and other products. Consumers are hit especially hard in the case of sugar and dairy products. In late 1984, the domestic price of sugar was four times the world price. Similarly, U.S. dairy product prices were two to three times the world price. The dairy program is also expensive to the taxpayer. In fiscal 1983, the treasury costs were $2.6 billion—or about $13,000 per commercial dairy farmer.[7] The cost of price supports, subsidized credit, and other USDA outlays is now roughly $50 billion per year and increasing rapidly. Farm programs are not an unmixed blessing to farmers. Farmers who rent or buy land, production rights, or other specialized resources, also face increased production costs.

The notion of individual rights, including the ability of people to engage in voluntary exchange is central to questions concerning the appropriate role of government in agriculture (and in other sectors). In the decentralized market process, maximum scope is provided for individual choice. Only through this approach can the nation's agricultural resources be used most economically serving the interests of farmers, consumers, and taxpayers alike. In agriculture, as in many other areas of economic activity, government might make its greatest contribution by attempting to do less. In the long run, noninflationary monetary and fiscal policies plus a more open economy would benefit agriculture far more than the network of costly action programs now in place.

1. *Agricultural Finance: Outlook and Situation Report*, ERS, AFO-25, U.S. Department of Agriculture, December 1984, p. 7.

2. *Ibid.*, p. 3.

3. Many of the points discussed below are elaborated upon in more detail in E. C. Pasour, Jr., "The High Cost of Farm Subsidies," Backgrounder No. 388 (Wash., D.C.: Heritage Foundation, Oct. 22, 1984) and E. C. Pasour, Jr., "The Free Market Answer to U.S. Farm Problems," Backgrounder No. 389 (Wash., D.C.: Heritage Foundation, October 30, 1984).

4. David H. Harrington, "Income and Wealth Issues in Commercial Farm and Agricultural Policy," pp. 145–153 in *Increasing Understanding of Public Problems and Policies—1984* (Oak Brook, Ill.: Farm Foundation, 1984), p. 147.

5. William G. Lesher, at the Conference on Alternative Agricultural and Food Policies and the 1985 Farm Bill, sponsored by the Giannini Foundation and Resources for the Future, Berkeley, California, June 11, 1984.

6. Bruce L. Gardner, *The Governing of Agriculture* (Lawrence, Kansas: Regents Press of Kansas, 1981), p. 118.

7. *Dairy: Background for 1985 Farm Legislation*, Economic Research Service, U.S. Department of Agriculture, Agricultural Information Bulletin No. 474, September 1984, p. 28.

9

Where There Was a Will—

by Jess Raley

Mr. Raley, a free-lance author, speaker, philosopher from Gadsden, Alabama remembers how it was in Appalachia in the early 1930s when government support payments were initiated. He also recalls what he designates as the "commodity" programs of food handouts to the poor and how the recipients of such largess began to lose their independence and respect. This article is from The Freeman *of December 1979.*

In America today there seems to be near universal awakening to the fact that something is wrong. Individuals in vast numbers are no longer inspired to excel in their respective fields of endeavor.

Business leaders fault labor, OPEC, government, imports, and employee apathy. Labor blames business, government, OPEC, and the low wages paid in exporting countries. Rank and file citizens generally believe government, OPEC, labor, business, and lousy working conditions to be the primary culprits. Government suspects business, OPEC, foreign ingenuity, lack of respect for the dollar abroad, and malingering personnel on production lines. (Labor controls too many votes to be faulted by those who have to stand for election from time to time.)

Every cognizant individual old enough to remember when the zest for life was, of necessity, honed to a fine edge is fully aware that the intangible known as the American will has, in fact, diminished perceptibly. The only thing I can't understand about the case of diminishing will—and it really bugs me—is so many people asking why.

One of the few things I know for an absolute certainty is why the American will (that seems to be the accepted term used, no doubt, to avoid complicated nomenclature) is less vivacious, aggressive, and steadfast than it once was—why so many individuals feel little, if any, responsibility for themselves, their job, family, and government. I know why because I was there when it happened, saw the seeds of irresponsibility planted and observed the first bitter fruits of that harvest.

Let me say at this point that I have never known or learned to think of an *average* person. The people I meet, get to know, learn to like or dislike, are all individuals and a surprisingly large number of them are by no means devoid of will. On the other hand relentless encroachment on freedom of choice, innumerable restrictive regulations on enterprise, and the fact that people have learned that losers, as well as those who never see the starting gate, have equal recourse to one or more government wealth-sharing program tends to, more or less, dull the once fine cutting edge of America's will to excel.

In January 1933 I found it necessary to drop out of school. Dad was having a difficult time just feeding the family so I decided to move to my granddad's farm in Appalachia where I could, hopefully, earn my own living. Being in my middle teens at the time, I even expected to save enough money to return to school.

The old farm was in a steep narrow valley and, except for a few small level plots, the productive soil had washed away many years before. This was not particularly important to me since I didn't have the means to cultivate the land anyway, but I did find innumerable ways to make a living. I learned to hunt and trap animals for their fur, dig medicinal roots, especially ginseng, and where to sell them; find and rob wild bees; pick and market wild berries; and numerous other ways to earn money.

As a matter of fact I had a ball in Appalachia, lived well after the first few weeks and actually accumulated enough in the process to return to school. I was, therefore, really just a transient who learned from the local residents what I needed to know to attain my appointed goal, and then I moved on.

Below the Poverty Level

Everyone in the area must have been well below poverty level if there was a poverty level in those days. But the people who lived in the larger valleys and owned more level land seemed to be doing fairly well. It was the real poor folk, however, who lived in the ridges and small eroded valleys where I was, and were almost as poor, that I came to know and admire. These were the hustlers who parlayed their meager crops with what they could earn from other sources to sustain their families. In my opinion—and I've had a love affair with anthropology since the fifth grade—man, living in an organized society, has never been more free and independent than those people were. They accepted full responsibility for themselves and their families; no one expected anything from a source other than their own efforts.

Sometime that summer the government programs started. An agent came through offering to pay farmers from eleven to twenty-one dollars an acre, depending on how good he judged their cotton to be, to plow up all or any part

of it. Most farmers plowed up some part of their crop. With cotton selling for about five cents a pound and the area's history of low productivity, it was the practical thing to do.

The difference in payment caused considerable resentment among neighbors, however, since in midsummer most farmers think their crop is as good as the best and better than the rest. I had put in a small crop that year after all by plowing for an elderly gentleman in exchange for the use of his mule and plow, a day for a day. Since I had only three acres of cotton, I didn't destroy any of it. I did get a preview, however, of how government programs would be administered when the agent paid his cousin top money for seven acres of very poor cotton while offering or paying at or near the bottom level to most everyone else.

The Commodity Program

Next came the commodity program designed by the "philanthropists" in Washington to feed the poor better than they could feed themselves while reducing the mountains of surplus commodities. The program seemed to work well in that it achieved these goals. No doubt its sponsors were quite pleased with themselves. But I still hurt when I remember what it did to most of the people who participated. In retrospect, these first ripples of government intervention were very small indeed in relation to the tidal waves that have followed. However, they were that first step of a long journey, a foot in the door that had heretofore been strictly private, the first pitch of a whole new ballgame.

At first only a few of the more indolent signed up to receive commodities. Then, as others saw their neighbors eating better without effort than they could eat by scratching as hard as they could, more and more people capitulated. It was like watching trees in a virgin forest fall and knowing they would never grow quite so tall again. Envy and resentment played a major role, along with nagging spouses. But for whatever reason, when individuals signed up for commodities they seemed to become different people, lose the essence of their zest for life.

Everyone in the area must have been eligible to receive commodities. At first, only a few signed up so the people who had accepted the job of distributing them were forced to get out and beat the bushes in an effort to find people who would take the mounting piles of food off their hands. I happened to be at a friend's house one day—we had cut a bee tree and were dividing the honey—when a commodity agent came by looking for prospects. He explained that the food was piling up and that he had to move it to hold his job. When we declined his offer the agent asked my friend pointblank why we refused; and I doubt to this day that a better answer could have been given.

"I don't do nigh as good a job supporting my family as I would like to do," he said, "but I well know whose job it is." That, I believe, is a classic example of the will, once so prevalent, that built America—the will so many people are hoping their fellow citizens can recapture in this age.

By the time I left Appalachia it was easy to detect participants in the commodity program just by talking with them. People who had been eager to help cut a bee tree, dig a load of rhododendron and ferns to sell, or any of the numerous projects that offered some small remuneration, were no longer interested after being on commodities for a while. More than this, their thinking changed perceptibly. Americans, since the Revolution, had felt responsible—not to government but for government—in the same sense that they felt responsible for themselves and their family. As individuals accepted or were forced to participate in various programs, they changed positions, in their own mind, placing government in the parent role of primary authority and responsibility. In less than two years, fully one-third of the people in the area were accepting government handouts in lieu of individual will.

The Sad Consequence

The things I saw happen in that remote region were, of course, being acted out in every nook and corner of these United States. As the years passed, more and more people became addicted to an ever-increasing number of government programs. Industrial workers protected by powerful unions with unrealistic contracts, obtained in many cases with the aid of government pressure, often do no more than dabble at their work. Extra effort and ingenuity is not necessary to hold a job; as a matter of fact, motivation is often frowned on by fellow workers where just drifting with the flow has become the norm. After all, if the company goes broke, the employees can always draw their pennies.

Since the stone of necessity no longer keeps a cutting edge honed on individual will the American economy has been forced to draw more and more on that reserve we hillbillies are wont to call gut fat—capital, labor, technology, and motivation invested before the American will was inhibited by government handouts and restrictions. In those days a man was responsible without recourse for his own house. He could invest his means in a business venture knowing that as the owner he could hire acceptable personnel, direct operations, enjoy the fruits of success, or suffer loss if the venture was a failure. The people employed by such a man knew they could do their job well and stay on the payroll, possibly moving to a better position if the business prospered; or they could fail to show incentive and find themselves terminated.

A long-time friend of mine has been associated with railroads all his working life. He and I were discussing this gut-fat proposition recently and he ventured the guess that if a railroad were built from scratch today, rights of way included, the builder having to contend with all the regulations and restrictions prevalent at this time, it would cost at least one hundred dollars to ship a peck of wheat

bran, on said railroad, from St. Louis to Chicago. No doubt my friend exaggerated somewhat, but I would be unwilling to promote such a project hoping to prove him wrong.

With American productivity deteriorating progresssively, rank and file citizens as well as leadership in government and business are voicing grave concern about the erosion of this element known as the American will. Even coming late in the game as it has, when our place in the sun is much less secure than it once was, this near universal awakening should be good for the country. I must admit, however, that I would be a great deal more elated if cognizant adults would quit "playing like" they don't know what's causing the trouble. This breed has been known to pour water on a drowned man in a sincere effort to revive him.

10

The Continuing Plight of Agriculture

by Dennis Bechara

Mr. Bechara is an attorney familiar with the history as well as the current rules and regulations of the farm program. He is a frequent contributor to The Freeman. *This article, from the May 1986 issue, is based on a lecture delivered at a FEE seminar.*

He exposes in detail the ramifications and the impact of the latest farm bill, in contrast to the Agricultural Adjustment Act of 1933. The ever-mounting burden of subsidies and taxes is quite intolerable.

On December 23, 1985, President Reagan signed into law the Food Security Act of 1985, commonly known as the "farm bill." This statute will affect the state of American agriculture for the next five years. During the past year, the precarious condition of the agricultural sector has been a hotly debated issue. Although the enactment of the 1985 farm bill is designed to confront and resolve the crisis, the unfortunate fact remains that the same failed tools which were utilized in the past will continue to be used in the future. It should not surprise us if more surpluses and low farm prices continue to plague the farm sector in the immediate future.

Why is our agricultural sector in such a precarious state? Is more government intervention the answer to the problem? Before analyzing our current crisis, it will be instructive to review our past agricultural policies, for our present attitudes toward the farm sector may be explained by our historical development as a country. Only if we fully understand the root of our policies will we be in a position to improve the lot of agriculture.

One of the fundamental differences between the development of the United States and the evolution of Europe is the abundance of land in this country. As the government acquired more land rights in the West, it became the national

policy of the country to settle the West and to actually give away land to those who were willing to carve a family farm out of the wilderness. The Homestead Act of 1862 is perhaps the watershed of this reality. It has been estimated that over one billion acres of land were thus given out to settlers during the settlement of the West.

Although most of the family-size farms essentially provided sustenance to the families that operated them, farmers were able to grow enough crops out of which they hoped to acquire other goods that they needed. The problem, however, was that as a result of the Federal farm policies, which encouraged anyone who wanted to enter farming to do so, a perennial surplus of production always loomed on the horizon.

As the newly settled farmers attempted to set up their operations, they faced innumerable obstacles. A significant one was the need for capital to finance their operations. Consequently, farmers, in general, became a debtor class. Politically, this meant that traditionally they favored a policy of easy credit and easy money. Perhaps because of the dispersed land ownership pattern that evolved as the West was settled, farmers also tended to regard any concentration of economic power with suspicion. They therefore generally favored both the regulation of railroads and the dismantling of large corporate utilities. Granges were partly responsible for the regulation of railroads on a state-by-state basis. These state laws, in turn, prompted Congress to enact the Interstate Commerce Act in 1887 which regulated railroads on a national scale.

Prior to the First World War, there was a farm surplus problem. However, as a result of the outbreak of the war, and the subsequent American participation in it, the federal government encouraged further agricultural production. Easy credit policies were enacted, and the justification for the overproduction was epitomized in the slogan "Food Will Win the War." Predictably, at the end of the war, farm prices fell, reflecting the government-encouraged surplus production. As protection to the farmers, Congress proceeded to enact higher tariffs on farm commodities through the McCumber Act of 1922. But farm prices remained low. Farming was perhaps the one bleak point in the economic boom of the 1920s. No matter what the government did, farm prices remained low.

Parity

The year 1922 saw the birth of the concept of "parity." This concept first appeared in a booklet written that year by George N. Peek and Hugh S. Johnson entitled "Equality for Agriculture." The thesis of this booklet was that farmers were entitled to receive a "fair" price for their commodities. The fairness of the price was connected to the level of prices received during the golden era of agriculture, which were the ten years that preceded the First World War.

Congress, reflecting the thinking of the farm sector, enacted proposals which embodied these ideas. The proposals were known as the McNary-Haugen bills. These bills would have restructured domestic distribution of farm commodities, so as to raise the prices to the much-heralded "parity" level. The excess which would not be marketed domestically, however, would have, in effect, been dumped on the international market while the U.S. consumer would have paid for this subsidy. These bills did not become law, and in 1927, when President Coolidge vetoed the latest version of these bills, he justified his veto utilizing rather prophetic language. In his veto message, the President said the following:

> Government price-fixing, once started, has alike no justice and no end. It is an economic folly from which this country has every right to be spared . . . There is no reason why other industries—copper, coal, lumber, textiles, and others—in every occasional difficulty should not receive the same treatment by the government. Such action would establish bureaucracy on such a scale as to dominate not only the economic life but the moral, social, and political future of our people. The main policy of this bill runs counter to the well-considered principle, that a healthy economic condition is best maintained through a free play of competition, by undertaking to permit a legalized restraint of trade in these commodities and establish a species of monopoly under government protection, supported by the unlimited power of the farm board to levy fees and enter into contracts. For many generations such practices have been denounced by law as repugnant to the public welfare. It cannot be that they would now be found to be beneficial to agriculture.

Agriculture in the 1920s experienced an unsurpassed productive capacity as the result of both technological advances and governmental policies. Naturally, farm prices had to decrease in view of this surge in productivity, and the signals that the low prices communicated to society were that there were too many resources invested in agriculture. The adjustment process has proven painful to many farmers. In 1790, 96 per cent of the population was engaged in farming. By 1927, the farming sector had decreased to 27 per cent. The farming sector is now one-tenth of what it was 50 years ago—2.5 per cent. Low farm prices were a symptom that indicated to society that its resources were misallocated and that a migration away from agriculture was the desired goal. In spite of all the government policies enacted to halt this migration, the trend has continued.

During Herbert Hoover's administration, prices received by farmers fell to historically depressed proportions. Farm income fell by more than half between 1929 and 1932. As a palliative, a new government agency was organized to take care of falling prices. This was the Federal Farm Board which was organized as a result of the Agricultural Marketing Act of 1929. Endowed with a revolving fund of $500 million, the Federal Farm Board set about to stabilize the prices of

wheat and cotton. The price of a bushel of wheat was $1.04 in 1929, but in spite of the purchasing activities of this agency, the price of wheat fell to 39 cents per bushel by 1931. The Board accumulated such large stocks of wheat, that at one point it controlled 80 per cent of the country's supply. Cotton fared no better. After having incurred heavy losses, Congress refused the agency any further funds and it ceased operations. Protectionism, however, seemed to be the course of action to follow, and the Smoot-Hawley Tariff of 1930 only succeeded in engendering further retaliatory tariffs that impeded world trade.

The New Deal

With the advent of the Roosevelt administration, a host of new statutes were enacted which were designed to treat the economic emergency caused by the Great Depression. Each sector of the economy provided its own explanation for the cause of the crisis. Agriculture too had an explanation for its problems: there was just too much production. So the Agricultural Adjustment Act of 1933 was enacted. This is the prototype of the legislation that in many ways is still in effect today.

The cornerstone of the Agricultural Adjustment Act of 1933 was to raise farm income by reducing production. Farmers were paid to reduce the acreage under cultivation and were guaranteed a minimum price on certain commodities. The crops that were to be controlled by this statute were the so-called "basic" commodities: wheat, corn, cotton, peanuts, rice, and tobacco. Although these commodities generated about one-fifth of farm income, they earned the lion's share of government funds spent in order to support prices.

One of the oddities of the price support system has been that it is designed to subsidize the volume of production, not the farmers' needs. Thus, small farmers have consistently received very few benefits from the price support system, whereas large farmers have benefited proportionally more. At the present time, one-third of all farms in the United States produce approximately 85 per cent of all farm sales. Therefore, two-thirds of all farmers receive insignificant government assistance from the price support system.

The implementation of the farm policy of the New Deal was mainly based on acreage reductions rather than on price supports, since these supports were set at a low level. However, with time, the support prices began to be increased to reach levels above the market-clearing point, so that stocks of surplus commodities began to appear. Land which produced subsidized crops was cultivated more intensely to increase the yield per acre. Other land that would have produced subsidized crops had it not been for the acre reduction requirement was cultivated for various additional crops. This, in turn, created surpluses in other areas as well.

The mechanics of the price support system have not changed very much since their inception in 1933. The Department of Agriculture, through an agency called the Commodity Credit Corporation (CCC), issues nonrecourse loans to farmers who produce the subsidized commodities. If the price of the commodity rises above the loan rate, the farmer is free to sell the commodity and is obligated to repay the loan. Therefore, the loan rate becomes a minimum price. If, on the other hand, the price of the commodity falls below the loan rate, the farmer simply relinquishes the commodity over to the CCC and the loan is considered paid in full. Thus, whenever the loan rate is set above market-clearing levels, the CCC ends up holding the surplus production.

Loans and Deficiency Payments

The Agriculture and Consumer Protection Act of 1973 introduced the concept of "deficiency payments," which consists of an additional subsidy representing the difference between the lower loan rate and the higher price support or price target. Farmers are entitled to a deficiency payment whenever the selling price of the regulated commodity falls below the price support point. Although designed to avert the chronic overproduction of agricultural commodities, the mechanism has proven ineffective in reaching its goals.

The 1985 farm bill has continued the use of both nonrecourse loans and deficiency payments. The only change is that the loan rate has been lowered in an attempt to control chronic overproduction. The purpose of the lower loan rate is to encourage farmers to sell their products in the marketplace rather than forfeiting them to the CCC. The anticipated lower farm income is supposed to be offset, however, by the deficiency payment. Therefore, since the farmer will still receive a subsidy, regardless of the market price of the commodity, it is doubtful that surpluses will be eliminated.

The export boom of the 1970s once more temporarily eliminated the perennial surplus problem. The government relaxed all production controls, and 55 million acres of cropland were added to production in order to meet this demand. Financial institutions, in turn, issued credit based on the assumption that land prices, which were increasing, provided sufficient collateral. Farm debt, which stood at $50 billion in 1970, increased to $214 billion by 1985. But after 1981 several factors radically altered the picture. Interest rates increased, a world recession reduced exports and other countries began to increase their productive capacity. In addition to this, the value of the dollar increased, making farm products even more expensive in the world markets.

Notwithstanding the massive subsidies farmers receive from the federal government, the farm economy is presently facing a severe crisis. Farm income has decreased by about a third during the past four years. In spite of this, the costs of the price support and market subsidies that form part of our national farm policy have ballooned to unprecedented levels. When the 1981 farm bill was

enacted, it was expected to cost the taxpayers no more than $12 billion. Instead, the actual costs incurred amounted to over $60 billion. Similarly, in 1981, farm exports reached the unprecedented height of $44 billion, which represented approximately 60 per cent of the world's agricultural market. Our share of the market has subsequently declined to approximately 50 per cent and our exports were $32 billion in 1984.

The 1981 price support legislation enacted rigid and high price supports which only encouraged other countries to further increase their production. Therefore, land values began to decline. Since the value of the collateral no longer supported more credit, financial institutions have reduced lending. Since 1981, around 200,000 farmers have gone out of business.

In light of the fact that the price support levels have been above market clearing levels, the government has acquired large stocks of the surplus production. As a temporary solution, in 1983 the "Payment in Kind" (PIK) program was designed. Farmers who participated in the scheme were given comparable amounts of crops. Eighty-three million acres of cropland were idled, and the government surplus disappeared. But sales of fertilizer, machinery, feed and other products necessary for farming were reduced. Experts at Georgia State University estimated that the PIK program cost 200,000 jobs. This estimate does not include the actual amount of crops given away, approximately $10 billion.

The 1985 farm bill continues substantially the same policies of the past. The outcome of past actions has consistently been overproduction. In response to the surplus problem, Congress has established four mechanisms to combat surpluses. These are the acreage reduction programs, marketing agreements, voluntary land retirement, and import quotas. The 1985 farm bill continues this trend.

The acreage reduction program goes hand-in-hand with the price support mechanism. Essentially, if a farmer wishes to participate in the subsidy program, he or she is required to limit the acreage apportioned to the cultivation of the subsidized commodities.

Marketing Orders

Marketing orders represent another mechanism for dealing with the recurrent surplus problem. The marketing order scheme has its origins in the Capper-Volstead Act of 1922 which allowed the formation of agricultural cooperatives. This statute exempted agricultural cooperatives from the coverage of the antitrust legislation. Even though the cooperatives were free to cartelize production, they were never able to effectively influence prices because not all producers agreed to join them. In other words, the forces of the market prevented the formation of monopolies. Therefore, further statutory intervention was required, which culminated in the Agricultural Marketing Agreement Act of 1937.

This statute authorized the Secretary of Agriculture to set up marketing orders for milk, vegetables, fruits and other minor products. Presently, there are 47 marketing orders in effect, covering a variety of crops worth around $5 billion a year. After a marketing order is adopted by the Secretary of Agriculture, a referendum of producers is held. If the order is ratified, it then comes into effect. The order may be amended from time to time by the Secretary, who usually follows the recommendation of producer administrative committees. Some of the marketing orders are not particularly important. For example, the market-support variety requires producers to contribute to an advertising fund. However, most of the marketing orders are designed to restrict supply in various ways. Some are concerned with setting quality standards. Others restrict the amount of products the farmer may bring to market, or determine how much fresh produce handlers may ship, or require producers to put part of their crop in storage until market conditions improve so as not to lower the market price. Any excess must be diverted for other uses, or simply left to waste.

Predictably, the effect of marketing orders is to increase prices. In addition, resources are misallocated since supply-control orders, by raising prices, encourage more production of the commodity. This, in turn, produces more waste, since more commodities are then diverted to other uses or left to rot. It has been estimated, for example, that up to 30 per cent fewer acres would be needed to produce the amount of California and Arizona oranges which ultimately are marketed. Innovation is also reduced, since there is no incentive to reduce costs of production because a producer's sales are limited by the orders. An example of an innovation that has been frustrated has been the development of a special shrink wrap that would allow lemons to be wrapped fresh for periods of about six months. It has also been estimated that 25 per cent of the lemon crop is wasted.

Voluntary land retirement has been a traditional method whose purpose has been to reduce agricultural production. In many instances, the additional purpose of fostering soil conservation has also been utilized as a means of limiting farm acreage. By the 1960s, 60 million acres had been removed from production. Ironically, the price support system and the disaster payment programs have encouraged farming in areas that have been subject to unusual environmental risks. For example, in the semi-arid climate of the Great Plains, ranchers may be tempted to cultivate some of the subsidized crops. After the prairie grasses are eliminated and a crop cultivated, the rancher may be required to set aside part of his land in order to receive the subsidies. This only exposes that soil to the dangers of erosion. The 1985 farm bill has recognized the deleterious effect of the price support system to certain erodible lands, and the eligibility of those lands in the subsidy program has been restricted.

Import quotas are the fourth method which has traditionally been used to

combat surpluses. Sugar is one of the products that has consistently been protected from foreign competition. The domestic price of sugar is approximately four times the world price. Foreign-grown sugar may only be imported in limited quantities and from certain countries. The sugar quota allowed from foreign countries has decreased significantly over the past four years. In 1981 we imported 5 million tons of sugar, whereas by 1985 the amount had decreased to 1 million. This has foreign policy repercussions, since most sugar-producing countries are less-developed countries that urgently need foreign exchange to support their economies.

Surplus Production

In spite of the operation of these four methods of reducing surplus production, the fact remains that the high price supports have consistently provided the incentive to engage in overproduction. If the price supports did not exist, farmers would guide production based upon market prices. When market prices are low, the signal communicated to producers is that production should be reduced. With the present system, however, farmers can disregard the market signals and overproduce, confident that the government will guarantee a maximum price. The surplus production only succeeds in lowering market prices, which, in turn, becomes the political justification for keeping the price support system in effect.

One of the justifications for price supports and marketing orders is that agriculture is a different type of industry. There are many aspects of the agricultural cycle that are beyond the control of farmers. Natural disasters, insect infestations and droughts are only an example of the difficulties with which farmers have to contend. But there is a large segment of agriculture, over half of the sector, which operates without the benefit of price supports. Livestock, as well as many fruits and vegetables, have successfully operated without these supports.

The free market has the capability of protecting farmers against unforeseen price fluctuations through the trading of agricultural options. This system enables farmers to sell a commodity sometime in the future at a predetermined price. Since 1936, however, this system had not been allowed to operate in most of the major domestic commodities. But as a result of the enactment of the Futures Trading Act in 1982, the trading of agricultural options in the regulated commodities has been allowed. The first trading of these contracts began in October 1984. It should be pointed out, however, that with the price support system in place, the prospects of these contracts are limited.

The current agricultural programs have inconsistent and conflicting effects. Some of the programs—like easy credit to buy and operate a farm, or research activities or irrigation projects—lower the costs of production. Other programs—some of the ones discussed in this article—tend to increase prices. Our legislated programs are encouraging overproduction, which has the unwanted effect of decreasing prices and reducing farm income. The surplus production which the federal government normally holds, has been partially sold in the international markets. Foreign countries have increased their productive capacity, and this alternative no longer is viable in the long run. Our farm policy should not be based on sheer hope that some future event will take care of overproduction.

Circumstances have changed over the past fifty years. Farm income, as a percentage of the income generated in urban areas, has increased. The farm sector, on the average, earns about four-fifths of the earnings in the non-rural sector. Politics should be eliminated from the formulation of our farm policy. It is not unknown for politicians to encourage the raising of price supports at strategically convenient times in order to gain votes. It is time we stop the present contradictory and negative farm policy. The longer we hesitate in embracing the free market, the worse it will be for all.

Part Three

International Implications

The domestic impact of the farm problem should be more than sufficient argument for rejecting the interventions and embracing once again the alternative of open competition. But that is by no means the end of the problem or the case against such controls. The essays in this section have to do with world hunger and the manner in which U.S. farm programs influence agricultural policies in other countries, especially in the socialist lands that so often are on the brink if not engulfed in widespread famine and starvation. From whatever perspective one views the situation, the sad and inevitable conclusion is that the more the U.S. government disrupts domestic and world prices of farm products the greater is the harmful impact on the least affluent farm producers and consumers of less developed lands.

11

A Pattern for Failure

by John Chamberlain

The Freeman'*s chief reviewer, John Chamberlain, touches again on the farm problem as he reviews in the May 1985 issue a book by Swedish economist Sven Rydenfelt,* A Pattern for Failure: Socialist Economies in Crisis. *In his study of "state planning" in more than a dozen countries of socialist leaning, Professor Rydenfelt sees the results in the form of crop failure and famine.*

I n *A Pattern for Failure: Socialist Economies in Crisis* (New York: Harcourt Brace Jovanovich, 175 pages), Sven Rydenfelt, a Swedish economist, offers a general proposition endorsed by Milton Friedman in a thoughtful introduction. The general proposition is that wherever there is detailed central economic planning the ordinary man suffers. The reason, says Rydenfelt, is ecological: people are dependent on their economic and social environments, and when individual entrepreneurs are discouraged by oppressive government-imposed constraints the creativity that feeds everybody languishes.

There is some elaboration of Rydenfelt's general thesis in an opening section devoted to the importance of the entrepreneurial environment. Like George Gilder in America, Rydenfelt thinks the supply of entrepreneurial incentive is more important than the supply of capital. If a man has a good idea, and there are no regulations to prevent him from pushing it, he will get the capital he needs somehow.

Once having established the outlines of his theory of the general importance of the entrepreneurial climate, however, Sven Rydenfelt rapidly shifts the emphasis of his book. What he is really interested in doing is to show how socialist governments mess up their agricultural policies, bringing starvation by their treatment of the peasants.

Communist and socialist governments, no matter how they come to power, are impelled by Marxist theory to favor the industrial proletariat. Partly this is due to Marx's own contempt for what he considered the stupidity of country life. Depending on the city workers to keep them in power, socialist governments fix the price they are willing to pay the peasants at a point that is low enough to guarantee cheap food to the urban masses. It doesn't matter whether the peasant keeps nominal title to his acres or not—the failure to let farmers sell their crops as they please reduces the incentive to produce. Peasants will normally work hard enough to keep their own families fed, but without market freedom there will be nothing extra to forestall possible famines.

Sven Rydenfelt's evidence, which is elaborately displayed, is that the famines always come. The pattern was set in Soviet Russia, when there was drought in the Ukraine in the years after the Bolshevik takeover. There wouldn't have been serious trouble if there had been a stored reserve. But the civil war had emptied the grain bins. Lenin used the weather as an excuse. But he was realistic enough to postpone agricultural collectivism.

Telling the peasants to enrich themselves—i.e., to become kulaks—he proclaimed the so-called NEP, or New Economic Policy. The theory was too successful to please Stalin, who, in the early Thirties, decided to break the power of the kulaks and establish big state farms. The result was a forced famine that killed some three million skilled agriculturalists.

Stalin in Charge

Stalin claimed successes for the new collectives, but when Khrushchev decided to expose the excesses of Stalinism, one of the first figures he revealed was that in 1953 Russia had fewer livestock than it had in 1913, when there were 60 million fewer people to feed.

In the long run Khrushchev proved to be no improvement on Stalin as a farm manager. His attempt to bring new acres under cultivation in semiarid areas worked out badly. Rydenfelt says there were crop failures in Russia in nine out of twenty years between 1963 and 1983. The excuse was always that the weather had been bad. The Communist high command solved the problem of the recurrent shortages by importing grain from the capitalist West.

Sven Rydenfelt follows his section on the failures of Soviet agricultural planning with chapters on what has happened to farming in Poland, Romania, Czechoslovakia, Yugoslavia, Hungary, Portugal, China, India, Vietnam, Sri Lanka, Ghana, Tanzania, Cuba, and Argentina.

In all cases save that of Hungary the courses followed by communist or "planning" governments have resulted in general impoverishment. The Hungarians have saved themselves by letting their peasants sell their produce in the open market. There is a repetitive quality to Sven Rydenfelt's story, but this is bone and marrow of the central point that he is determined to drive home.

Rydenfelt's examples do not include Ethiopia, Angola, Mozambique, Chad, and the general sub-Saharan region in Africa. But we know from the news stories that there are no exceptions to Rydenfelt's rule that, where socialism prevails, starvation is just around the corner.

12

African Famine: The Harvest of Socialist Agriculture

by David Osterfeld

The study by Professor Rydenfelt, covered in the preceding essay, failed to include a chapter on the drought and famine in Ethiopia. In the October 1985 Freeman *that omission was covered by Dr. Osterfeld, Associate Professor of Political Science at St. Joseph's College, Rensselaer, Indiana. It is the same old pattern of marketing boards, protectionism, state farms, land reform, and ultimate failure.*

The popular explanation of the current famine in Africa is the drought. But is this convincing? The North American Great Plains has major droughts about every twenty years, the most severe being the 1934–36 Dust Bowl. A major drought was recorded in California in 1977 and the 1975–76 drought in England was labeled "unprecedented" in its severity. Yet none of these resulted in famine. In fact, the 1977 California harvest was a record high. And food production in England increased by 15 per cent between 1975 and 1980.

Why is it that droughts occur in all parts of the world but, with a few exceptions, famines are confined to Africa?

The United Nations (UN) has listed 24 African countries as threatened by famine. These countries have one crucially important thing in common. They have all pursued policies which amount to nothing short of an assault on agriculture. The policies include the following.

Marketing Boards—The stated purpose of these Boards, which are found in most of the 24 countries including Ethiopia, is to insulate the farmer from price fluctuations. In fact, the Boards are typically used to raise government revenue. The farmer is forced to sell his produce to the Board which, because it is a government monopoly, need pay him only a fraction of its actual market value. The typical farmer in Tanzania receives about 10 per cent of the value of his produce. In Kenya it is 15 per cent and in Ghana 20 per cent. Adding insult to injury, the farmer must then pay taxes on the income he does receive.

Outlawing Middlemen—The Boards could not operate as revenue agents if farmers were free to sell their produce elsewhere. Thus, the private sale of food has been outlawed or severely restricted in many countries. In Ethiopia and Tanzania, for example, those caught violating the prohibition are beaten or killed.

Protectionism—In order to stimulate local industry and to appease a small but politically powerful urban elite, private foreign investment has been discouraged and foreign-owned companies have been nationalized. Tariffs, subsidies and licensing restrictions have been enacted. These policies have allowed local manufacturers to sell their goods at well above free market levels. This means that the African farmer must confront artificially inflated prices with an artificially deflated income.

State Farms—State farms are notoriously inefficient. While other socialist countries such as China have been dismantling them, African countries have been busy creating them. Ghana established large state farms in the 1960s. Its per capita food output fell 19 per cent during the 1970s. Tanzania began its Ujama Program in 1970, resettling some 13 of its 18 million people onto collective villages. Its per capita food output fell 15 per cent in ten years. A food exporter in 1970, it imported over $16 million worth of food in 1980. Mozambique became independent in 1975 and promptly created state collectives. Within 5 years per capita food output fell 12 per cent. In Ethiopia state farms comprise 4 per cent of the land, receive 90 per cent of the state's agricultural investment, but 80 per cent of them operate at a loss. Yet the ten-year plan calls for a doubling of the state farm sector.

Land Reform—Several countries, including Mozambique, Zaire, and Tanzania, have implemented land reform, but Ethiopia's is the best known. Contrary to the way it is depicted by the media, much of Ethiopia is extremely fertile. It would be the breadbasket of Africa, agronomists said, were its development not retarded by feudalism. In 1975 the new Marxist government nationalized all land. Feudalism ended; ''Ethiopian Socialism'' began. Instead of development, farm output, low to begin with, declined. Why? The principle of land distribution was to allocate to each family enough land to feed itself but no more. The use of hired labor was prohibited, as was the private sale of farm produce and machinery. The primary purpose of the reform said the UN, which applauded it as "progressive" and "forward-looking," was to prevent the emergence of "commercial agriculture" by making farm plots too small for machinery to be economically viable. Thus, the reform changed little. Under feudalism the farmer had little incentive to produce. Under socialism he has even less. Over 60 per cent of Ethiopia is arable. But only 10 per cent is cultivated. As one authority commented: "The low rate of land use may be attributed to lack of motivation to produce anything beyond subsistence levels."

It is hardly surprising that these policies produced shortages. Indeed, it would have been surprising if they had not.

The Market Solution

History shows two things quite clearly: 1) the application of Socialist measures to agriculture results in declining production, food shortages and sometimes even famine; and 2) the application of capitalist measures to agriculture tends to produce agricultural abundance.

For example, prior to the 1917 Revolution, Russia was a major exporter of food. By 1920, however, the area under cultivation in the Soviet Union had declined by 50 per cent and yields per acre fell by 40 to 50 per cent. An estimated six million Russians died of starvation. Millions more died in the 1930s as a result of Stalin's collectivization program. Eventually single-acre private plots were grudgingly permitted. Small as they are, these plots are about *40 times* as efficient as the collective farms. There is certainly a degree of irony in the fact that despite its tremendous agricultural potential the Soviet Union is now the single largest purchaser of U.S. grain exports.

India provides a very instructive contrast to the Soviet Union. After highly interventionist if not socialist policies resulted in famine in the early 1970s, India abandoned price controls on agriculture. By 1977 India not only was self-sufficient, it was exporting large quantities of grain. In addition, it had built up a grain reserve of 22 million tons, which enabled it to manage the severe drought of 1979 without the need for food imports.

The famine in Africa is certainly a tragedy. It is all the more tragic because it need not have happened. There is no need for it to happen again. Anyone with a serious desire to end recurrent famines would do well to take a look at what results from an ideological commitment to socialism. Let the free market operate, for wherever farmers have been exposed to market incentives, farm output has increased.

13

The Failure of International Commodity Agreements

by Karl Brandt

Long before the OPEC oil cartel, there were other international commodity agreements. Dr. Brandt was especially interested in those having to do with farm products such as wheat, coffee, sugar. In his address as a foreign member of the Académie d'Agriculture of France on May 27, 1964, subsequently printed in The Freeman, *he reviewed the history and foretold the future of past, present, and new cartels yet to be attempted. Again, the market affords the more hopeful alternative.*

I t is, if I am not mistaken, the goal of all free countries with government by law to diminish poverty, squalor, and drudgery for the greatest number of their citizens, and to expand opportunities to all self-respecting, responsible citizens to develop their personal potential. This goal includes the obligation of the nation to respect the dignity and integrity of all men of good will.

If this national goal is accepted, the economy must have the institutional framework to promote the gradual improvement of the real income of the people by improving the productivity of human, natural, and manmade resources. This requires, in the production of goods and services, more division of labor, specialization, and increased efficiency from research, innovation and better management. But in order to have some orientation for such endeavor it is essential to give the consumer the sovereign power to allocate resources to the satisfaction of his needs and of his more and more refined wants. This provides the powerful incentive to all people to make the effort to earn the money to get the goods and services they want. Such an arrangement is ideally guaranteed in the market with freely moving prices by the daily plebiscite in which housewives and the consumer in general express their preference in francs and centimes, or dollars and cents.

In the modern economy, in which this allocation of resources applies to all goods, durable and nondurable, to houses and motor vehicles, and to all services—educational, medical, culinary, artistic, and to entertainment, travel, insurance, recreation, and multitudes of others—economic growth is bound to accelerate and to become all-pervasive. Such dynamic growth, to be stable and continuous, requires a high degree of mobility of human resources, such as shifts from the production of goods to the performance of services.

Such economic growth or development, which requires above all stability of the national currency and the discipline of monetary and fiscal policies to keep inflation in check, calls also for an optimum of foreign trade. It is generally agreed that the promotion of peaceful relations in this turbulent and dynamic world requires economic development in all countries, particularly those with still predominantly rural living conditions. This development in formerly colonial and other industrially retarded countries is definitely needed for the healthy development of the advanced nations, because industrial economies maintain growth and stability by a reliable flow of essential raw materials.

The Need for Leadership

Of all the conditions for increasing the income of the people in the world's rural countries, by far the most strategic are continued healthy and stable growth of the leading industrial countries and their avoidance of prolonged economic stagnation or contraction. Any idea of accelerating growth in underdeveloped countries by sapping the strength of industrial nations belongs in the moth-eaten fabric of ideas of Marxian determinism and the *fata morgana* of the dictatorially-ruled "paradise for all proletarians." Since these grand ideas have been tried for close to 40 years in a laboratory experiment with several hundred million people, they have lost their luster and gaudy colors.

Today, the economies of industrial and developing countries are mutually interdependent, as is the guardianship of peaceful cohabitation of nations. Hence, while the industrial countries need an adequate and growing flow of primary material from developing countries, they will pay for these, as well as for manufactured goods from light industries, by exporting to those countries an increasing volume of manufactured producer and consumer goods, and will also help them to industrialize gradually.

If this mutually beneficial exchange is to flourish, all nations must act in accordance with their optimal comparative advantage, i.e., the opportunity to produce and sell at lower unit costs. To let this principle work requires optimal diminution or removal of hindrances to trade expansion, not only import quotas and customs duties but the whole arsenal of nontariff impediments in lieu of duties.

All the proposed solutions have one common denominator. They suggest that, by setting up international and regional world-wide administrative machinery to control and regulate prices for optimal financial liquidity of developing countries, the pace of raising the income of the poorest people in the most agrarian countries can be accelerated at will, and that more perfect equity and justice in distribution among independent nations can be attained.

A Dubious Device

Perhaps the most persuasive and yet the most dubious proposal to remedy the instability of foreign exchange earnings of developing countries is the device of international commodity agreements, abbreviated in the literature as ICA. This form of intervention in the international market for primary commodities is an excellent example that makes clear where the generating power originates that drives a national economy, and how complex and delicate a self-adjusting system the market economy actually is. When I speak of the market economy, I do not mean a laissez-faire system with no rules, but a competitive private enterprise economy with effective enforcement by the government of regulations, quality standards, and rules for competition.

International commodity agreements are arrangements between contracting governments, aimed at preventing precipitous price declines of a primary commodity on the world market, in order to avoid serious balance of payment and illiquidity problems for the governments of the exporting countries. But the attempt to forestall disastrous price declines also demands that brakes be put on too steeply rising prices, because such increases may unduly stimulate expansion of production, with resulting sharp price declines later.

This remedy for price instability consists basically of a type of market intervention that was adopted in the late twenties and early thirties on the European continent, in the United States, and in other parts of the world: farm income support through guaranteed minimum prices for specified agricultural commodities. These price support policies amount to a compulsory government-controlled cartel, with innumerable variations in detail. Since more than 30 years of experience with this policy have accrued in the industrially advanced countries and in the world market, it is relevant for our discussion to summarize the *modus operandi* and the economic results of this remedial counteraction to price instability.

Once the government supports the price of a commodity, the price can theoretically still move, but only above the so-called "floor" or guaranteed minimum. By political compromise this level is deliberately set above equilibrium, which by definition is the price that would clear the market. The politically set level is meant to be remunerative to the high cost or marginal producers, the low income farmers on whose behalf price stabilization is mainly established. It is therefore unavoidable that the price, and the elimination of any risk of its change by government guarantee, will act as a forceful incentive, especially to efficient producers, to expand the area for the specific crop. To counteract this the government imposes an area limit, the so-called "acreage allotment." Some sort of base is needed for its determination; usually a historical base is chosen, such as each farmer's actual average acreage of the crop cultivated in several base years. However, the common experience in all countries is that the combination of a profitable guaranteed price with the acreage allotment acts as a still more effective incentive for increasing output per unit of land on limited acreage by more intensive farming. More fertilizer, better seed, more irrigation, better pest and weed control, more cultivation, and various other methods are used. Hence, the government has to buy and store more grain to keep the price at the support level.

The Sorry Results

Up to this point the results of this intervention are already remarkable:

1. There is no longer any mobility of the geographical location of production. It is frozen from the moment the allotments are established.

2. The unintentionally subsidized intensification of production has created surpluses that exceed effective demand.

3. Therefore, the government has to finance and operate storage of commodity stockpiles.

4. Hence, the government at taxpayers' expense has entered the commodity business.

5. The price can no longer move upward but is tightly pinned to the "floor." Instead of a price support or the guarantee of a minimum price, one has a fixed, totally inflexible price.

6. This fixed price still governs producers, processors, everybody in the trade chain, and consumers. The price signals are set in false position for all of them. Although an excess supply exists, everybody can act only according to the price which indicates shortage, namely by consuming less, by substituting other commodities. The processors and the speculative trade reduce stock carrying because the government keeps the excess stocks at public expense.

7. In other words: without any intent to do so, the government has socialized stock carrying.

8. As a further result, the most effective commodity price and supply stabilizing institution, the commodity exchange with its trading in future delivery contracts, is made idle.

However, even those are by no means all the side effects. The Treasury has to pay for moving the commodity into and out of storage and for storing it, as well as for losses when the surplus is disposed of. Thus, there are innumerable secondary beneficiaries of stockpiling excess output, such as railroads, truckers, labor union members, and many others. All these receivers of windfalls acquire a vested interest in maintaining farm price supports. Much worse is the fact that the market in farm real estate discounts the subsidy-earning value of the acreage allotment. Hence, price stabilization of farm products boosts the value of farm land; in due time higher land prices and rents on leased land increase the costs of farming and force more intensive use. This is another unintentional side effect.

Marketing Quotas Assigned

When the excess production begins to bleed the Treasury too badly, the next step is to tighten the cartel by efforts to control the supply in the market. In addition to the acreage allotment the government imposes on all farms a marketing quota, which is established by subdividing a national quota prorated in accordance with individual acreage allotments. This national quota is fixed by a precarious government estimate of how large the domestic consumption and the net export may be one year later. Since the marketing quota tends to be smaller than the output, it immediately poses the problem of a black market and the necessity of suppressing it by heavy penalties. Output that exceeds the marketing quota can be stored, converted, or consumed by the farmer, but it cannot be marketed legally. Even in countries with a customarily law-abiding farm population, the temptation to profit by disposing of such illegal supply by barter or other black deals is strong, and actual enforcement is difficult.

The cartel price-fixing for agricultural commodities also unintentionally subsidizes increased production of the same commodity in other countries. Price-fixing thus creates effective competition abroad. Since it is politically unpopular and difficult to lower the guaranteed price level even when costs of production are declining, stabilization by political decision is practically identical with "stabilizing upward."

Finally, the greatest ordeal for the government agency responsible for operating the cartel is the obligation to dispose of the accumulated excess stocks so as not to undermine the fixed price. Such disposal would be simple if it were done by destroying the supply. Grain could be burned or dumped in the ocean, although even this costs money. But powerful social, moral, and political taboos prevent this solution for any major nonperishable food commodity. Only in the case of coffee in Brazil was destruction used as a market-corrective action. Therefore, the government must seek to release the excess of staple food commodities in foreign countries as gifts, on credit, or with lowered prices. Except for the gifts, this amounts to dumping, and has a deleterious impact upon producers in the recipient country, and secondarily on the exporting country's foreign markets and on its foreign economic relations.

It is a psychological fact that a commodity kept off the market by a government, in quarantine, so to say, is still a powerful factor influencing both the price and the actions of all parties in the market. Grain "in jail" is still grain, because if it is not destroyed it will in due time appear as market supply.

No Place To Hide

National commodity markets are a remarkably effective system of communicating vessels in which millions of interested consumers, retailers, wholesalers, speculators, and farmers keep the flow going. The idea of inserting into the market, via detours, major quantities of supply, under perfect quarantine or segregated from the ordinary supply, belongs in the realm of fiction. Only private charity distribution can minimize the impact on the market. Even the ably administrated food stamp plan of the late thirties in the United States proved that free food did not cause additional consumption of food, but actually subsidized consumption of other goods and services. To change the determined consumer's preference in his family budget decisions takes far more than free distribution of goods, the more so the poorer and prouder he is.

The cartel operation produces still other undesirable side effects. In many instances, particularly for industrial raw material products in agriculture such as cotton, jute, hemp, and sisal, the raised fixed price gives the greatest incentive to producers of substitutes. This exerts pressure on consumption of the original product, say cotton, at the expense of the farmer, whose marketing quota will be cut if national consumption shrinks.

The industrial temperate zone countries, which make a virtue out of the backwash of domestic political necessity and subsidize exports of agricultural raw materials such as cotton, thereby slide to the next necessity of granting more subsidies. Manufacturers of cotton textiles, who have to compete in the foreign market as well as in the domestic one, now need a subsidy to restore equal raw material costs. And so there are three recipients of subsidies: the farmer; the exporter of the farm product; and the manufacturer who uses the raw material.

However, I have not nearly exhausted the appalling record of unforeseen and unwanted distortions of economic processes caused by government intervention that attempts to remedy instability of commodity prices. Subsidized surplus disposal by gifts diverted to other countries can assist private charity that reaches the destitute, the sick, and helpless widows and orphans. But it cannot cure the causes of poverty. Only increased productivity on farms, in craftshops, in factories, and in the wholesale and retail trade can do that. It is here that the disposal of surpluses from abroad does its greatest harm. The majority of people in underdeveloped countries are small farmers who earn their cash income by selling farm commodities. Dumping such commodities in their market may be a boon to some of their customers in the cities, but the farmers resent it, and it diminishes the incentive for them to produce more.

I have yet to give the reasons why I believe that, whatever action may be taken to mitigate the impact of unstable commodity prices on the balance of payments of developing countries, the International Commodity Agreement method is not only inadequate and dubious but outright harmful to the best interests of the developing countries and to world trade in general. Basically, the sobering experience of sovereign governments of advanced nations with this enigmatic cartel policy in their national markets applies also to the immeasurably more difficult situation in the international commodity market.

One Control Leads to Others

The worst feature of all market intervention with price fixing is that, while dealing with one commodity or a few closely related commodities, this inevitably changes the relations between the price of the regulated commodity and the prices of all other commodities and services. The insertion of one rigid price into a range of flexible prices for some 160 or 170 agricultural products is like a boy who knows nothing about the meaning or the effects of the different positions turning switches at the control board of an automated factory. The far-reaching adjustments that farmers and all other affected parties must make to the accidental price relationships caused by fixing the price of one commodity are unpredictable. Therefore, such isolated treatment of the price mechanism for one country contributes more uncertainty tomorrow than there was instability prior to price fixing. The case for all such trouble-multiplying cures rests on the assertion that the adjustment of supply and demand under the rule of flexible prices does not function—an assertion that contradicts all evidence and economic experience.

The intent of stabilization is realized so long as the stabilization is upward. When, however, larger stocks have been accumulated and their disposal is unavoidable, the same consequences arise as in the case of price supports in domestic markets. Necessity commands that besides regular commercial sales, concessional sales be undertaken, or part of the supply be given away. This procedure leads to serious disorganization and corrosion of markets. The United States, with $6 billion worth of agricultural exports (1964), disposes of over 30 per cent in the form of concessional deals. This is not done on principle. Far from it. It is simply the accumulated backwash of an ill-chosen method of social income support.

Enforcement of ICA regulations is even more difficult than is enforcement in single countries. When one begins to speak of "policing the markets of coffee beans," I wonder how one dares suggest the feasibility of such control in vast areas where the United Nations is faced with the problem of preventing the murder of rural people by armed bands.

Problems of the Board

Aside from the dubious state of effective government administration, a serious question is whether competing countries can possibly agree on export or production quotas and thus freeze the geographical location of production, or administer shifts in location. The board of an ICA must try to achieve principles of equity and justice for all signatory parties to the multigovernment cartel. Originally, commodity agreements included exporting countries only and thus represented producer interests exclusively. They led to defensive policies by importing countries and their effect was nullified. Naturally, the enthusiasm of producers diminished as consumers won equal representation on ICA boards. Yet, without importing governments, such cartels are doomed.

Today, all such agreements include major importing as well as exporting countries. This demands far more wisdom than the fairest and ablest board possesses. Suppose one exporter earns 80 per cent of foreign exchange from the commodity, another 20 per cent. When quota restrictions are necessary to raise the price, will the exports from both countries be cut by the same percentage? If not, what principle shall determine the degree of discrimination and the number of years it shall last? If drastic changes in costs of production or handling or transportation of the regulated commodity occur, which apply to one or more countries but not to all, shall all nevertheless receive the same price? If the commodity comprises a range of qualities, with lower grades produced at disproportionately lower costs, shall quotas treat all the same? Such questions indicate that ICA's are bound to end up with all kinds of soft political compromises on the main points of control over supply, and even of price arrangements.

As soon as there is a serious contingency of substitution for the commodity by other natural, processed, or synthetic products, ICA price stabilization begins to sound the death knell for the original commodity. I indicated earlier that in many cases price supports operate, via detours of economic processes, to the long-run detriment of the cartelized producers. To prove my point that ICA's may become deadly poison I have only to mention the cases of rubber, wool, linseed oil, or tungnut oil.

Natural rubber was one of the commodities on which price stabilization ideas were tested in a world-wide experiment under Dutch and British management. The attempted producer-exporter cartel was mainly instrumental in pushing rubber plantations into other tropical areas, in stimulating experiments with other latex-yielding crops, and in boosting synthetic production of plastomers with large government subsidies in industrial countries. To kill the remaining industrial use of linseed oil, tungnut oil, or soybean oil, one need only fix the prices internationally.

Existing Agreements

Five ICA's are at present (1964) in existence: on wheat, sugar, coffee, olive oil, and tin. Only four, excluding olive oil, are important. The one for wheat is proclaimed by its supporters the outstanding success. It can be proved beyond discussion that the ICA's for wheat, sugar, and coffee amount to no more than sanctimonious declarations of good intentions. They have neither stabilized the incomes of the exporting countries nor avoided the whole range of unintentional distortions of world trade that do far more harm than good. Insofar as the wheat agreement has given some semblance of stabilizing price—though not income— it was due to the fact that the governments of the United States and Canada shouldered the burden of carrying the gigantic excess stocks. But both governments have had to enter into a multitude of noncommercial disposal arrangements that violate the principles of truly competitive international trade.

There is one little defect in all plans for administering economic progress at specified growth rates, which the econometricians usually fail to mention: no genius, no power in this world, has the ability to forecast the future supply, the demand, or the price for any commodity, or to predict the performance of one or of many national economies one, three, or five years from now. The most fabulous computers have not changed this situation one bit. We now know much faster and more accurately what has happened up to today. But as to the future, we get the wrong guesstimates also much faster, and with more scientistic trimming.

Restrictive compulsory cartel policies that raise prices to benefit high cost producers and artificially throttle output and supply to maintain such arbitrarily fixed prices, belong in the tool chest of the static society and its dirigism. Such policies are technically possible, but they are the antithesis of what the dynamic economy of an open and free humane society requires.

I expect much sound development in those primary material exporting countries that succeed in taming the monster inflation and, relying on their producers' ability to compete, pave the way for sound private investment of foreign capital, as the transfer of funds from government to government diminishes.

14

The Right to Food

by E.C. Pasour, Jr.

In his essay in the previous section, Professor Pasour reviewed the impact of U.S. farm policies on the farmers and the consumers of this nation. Here, from The Freeman *of April 1976, is his study of the problem of world hunger and why there can be no valid claim of an unearned right to food, or whatever, at home or abroad, by those who bring to the market nothing of value to exchange for that which they claim.*

People in the U.S. and throughout the world now have a heightened awareness of the age-old problems of hunger and poverty. It has been estimated that 460 million people throughout the world today suffer from acute malnutrition. At the same time, capacity to produce food is at an all time high in the U.S. and throughout the highly developed countries. Increasingly, questions are being raised about the apparent injustice of this coexistence of hunger and affluence.

The movement to provide more food to hungry people throughout the world has increased significantly since the early 1970's. The 1974 World Food Conference in Rome took what many regarded as an essential first step. The conference adopted an objective that within a decade no child will go to bed hungry and that no family need fear for its next day's bread. In the same spirit, a "Right to Food" resolution was introduced in both houses of the U.S. Congress in 1975. This resolution declares that every person in the U.S. and throughout the world has the right to a nutritionally adequate diet. The resolution has received the official sanction of various religious groups. Members of the Lutheran Church in America, for example, have been exhorted to contact their Representatives and Senators to "urge its passage."

The concerned citizen cannot be oblivious to his neighbor's condition. The fact that a problem exists, however, does not imply that all possible solutions are either feasible or right. What should be the attitude of the morally sensitive person toward this (or any other) "Right to Food" resolution? Do we, as individuals, have an obligation to support this legislation? More generally, what should be our stance toward world hunger problems? What can we as individuals do to alleviate the hunger problem facing half a billion people throughout the world?

The purpose of this paper is to analyze the "Right to Food" resolution. In doing so, the legitimacy of the right to food by citizens in the U.S. and in other countries will be discussed. The distinction between public and private charity will be stressed. Finally, limitations of charity as a long-run solution to hunger and poverty will be described.

The Concept Examined

There can be no universal right to food. The concept of the right to food cannot be supported on either economic or moral grounds. First, consider the economic implications of the right to food. The right to food basically involves the problem of income distribution. Food is man-produced. Proposals which assume a right to food (or income) by individuals within or outside the U.S. imply that there is no relationship between the incentives of food producers and food production. Many of the countries in which the hunger problem is most acute have attempted to ignore this relationship.

The right to food is fundamentally no different than a right to housing, clothing, and the like. Thus, there can be no economic bill of rights assuring everyone a specified level of "necessities," since dividing income differently will affect the output of goods and services and, consequently, the amount of income to divide. That is, the more equal the income distribution, the less enthusiasm there will be on the part of individuals to engage in wealth-producing activities.

Food and other goods must be produced before they can be distributed. This is just as true for a highly developed modern economy as it was for Robinson Crusoe. The absurdity of the concept of "Right to Food" is obvious in the case of a Crusoe economy. The same basic problem remains, however, for a modern economy. There is no way to legislate prosperity for all.

The recent bankruptcy of New York City is a predictable outcome of an attitude by public officials which holds that "we will not be constrained by economics in caring for our citizens." The minimum wage provides another good example of attempting to increase incomes by ignoring economic principles. Increases in the minimum wage cannot be used as a device to insure a minimum amount of income for all. Instead, the evidence in scores of examples has shown that the effect of an increase in the minimum wage is to eliminate jobs for marginal workers—not to increase their income.

Though a policy which is not feasible from an economic standpoint could hardly be moral, there are other moral objections to any universal right to food. Any right to a given level of food must be at someone else's expense. Granting individual A the right to food (or any other good) means that an obligation is simultaneously being imposed on person B to provide the food since food must be produced to be consumed. Any right for one individual which imposes an unchosen obligation on other individuals can hardly be regarded as a moral right. This point is closely related to the distinction between "public" and private charity.

Public vs. Private Charity

Charity by its very nature implies a voluntary, freely chosen act. However, the "Right to Food" resolution involves not private charity but an involuntary gift of food (and income) from people who are not disposed to provide such aid. The "Right to Food" resolution involves the use of the state's power to collect from individuals more than they are willing to contribute privately. Any individual is now free to contribute privately as much as he chooses for domestic and foreign relief agencies. The "Right to Food" resolution means, however, that individuals should be forced to contribute more to such work than they freely choose.

Support of legislation to coerce individuals into performing or abstaining from particular actions is inconsistent with the Judaeo-Christian concept of freedom. Blue Laws, prohibition, and anti-pornography provide other recent examples of legislation attempting to coerce individuals into particular modes of behavior. Freedom involves choice, not necessity, but means little if man is not free to choose—to choose good as well as evil. Thus, it is difficult to understand why a religious imprimatur should be placed on legislation intended to coerce individuals into supporting a particular activity. Such legislation will inevitably restrict the individual's freedom of choice.

The act of supporting legislation affecting income levels on moral grounds raises a host of questions—theoretical and practical. Numerous groups, some preponderantly low income (e.g., elderly) and some preponderantly high income (e.g., doctors and lawyers), use or attempt to use the power of the state to affect their incomes. What moral basis can one use to determine whether the income of a particular individual or group is too high or too low? The Aristotelian idea of a "just price," meaning anything other than the competitive market price, has long been discredited. The idea of a "just wage" determined administratively is just as spurious. The market provides only the objective basis for determining what the wage of a particular individual should be.

In reality, the incomes of most groups are influenced by the political process. Decisions to increase school teacher salaries or the level of social security benefits for the elderly, for example, are made in the political arena and reflect the political power of their individual constituencies. However, we have no objective basis apart from market forces for determining the "just" level of income for these or any other groups. The fact that individuals or groups have no moral basis for attempting to coerce other individuals into involuntary acts does not mean, of course, that the hunger problem is not worthy of our attention as individuals. We cannot be oblivious to problems of hunger and malnutrition within the U.S. or in less-developed countries. Private charity is an important activity and can often play a key role in alleviating distress. Unfortunately, the impulse for private charity and the individual's concern for his fellow man is being reduced by the progressively larger role of "public charity."

Right to food resolutions also have a pernicious effect in fostering expectations which, aside from problems of economic scarcity, are incapable of being fulfilled. There is no way to assure everyone the right to a nutritionally adequate diet or to insure, as proposed at the Rome Conference, that "no human being's future and capacities will be stunted by nutrition." Nutrition problems exist in all countries for persons at all income levels. All parents know that providing the proper food does not guarantee that a nutritious meal will be eaten. Interest in "Weight-watchers" and other diet programs indicates that practical difficulties associated with eating properly (even when food is abundant) are not limited to children.

Alternatives

For most of the world's hungry people, however, the basic problem is to obtain enough food. The question is not whether the plight of hungry people should be alleviated, but how. If the "Right to Food" resolution is not the proper approach toward alleviating hunger, what should we as individuals do? There is certainly a key positive role for private charity. Such aid can perform a valuable role in providing temporary relief in case of earthquakes, floods, and other disasters.

Western "imperialism," lack of resources and weather are being used as scapegoats by many underdeveloped countries to hide the effects of their own mismanagement. The advantage of abundant resources can easily be negated by government policies (as in Jamaica). On the other hand, Hong Kong, Singapore, South Korea and Taiwan demonstrate the fact that resource-poor areas can develop when economic incentives are present. The fact that Russian farmers produce 25 per cent of their food in private plots worked by farmers in their spare time provides additional evidence of the effect of economic incentives on output.

The only long-run solution to low income and hunger is to increase the output of the people involved, since wages depend primarily on the productivity of labor. For a given economic system, the productivity of labor depends on the amount of resources, including machinery and equipment available to work with. Increasing the ratio of capital to labor requires incentives to invest and produce.

Yet, many of the underdeveloped countries fail to provide the climate for economic development, with an overt hostility toward a system of economic incentives.

Attempts to avoid the "mistakes" of a market economy through comprehensive central planning in "Third World" countries are almost certain to impede economic development. There are no short cuts to economic development or panaceas to solve low-income and hunger problems. Capital formation requires time, and hasty decisions adversely affecting investment by domestic and foreign investors can affect the lives of a country's inhabitants for decades to come. The shortages, "bottlenecks" in production, low emphasis on output of consumer goods, and the like in Russia and other centrally directed economies are predictable results of relying on central control instead of the market in organizing economic activity. The typical person has little appreciation of the way in which the price system of a market economy provides information to market participants. For example, the amount of information required and number of decisions involved in getting a loaf of bread into a consumer's hands is staggering to contemplate.

Though charity may alleviate some temporary distress problems, the only long-run answer to world hunger and low income lies fundamentally within the countries themselves. Neither private nor "public" charity is an effective substitute for basic political and economic reforms. Good intentions are not enough. "Right to Food" resolutions, whether passed or not, are likely to have a harmful effect on development efforts, since they divert attention from the basic problem. If enacted, such resolutions may also impede long-run development by enabling developing countries to adopt policies which discourage capital formation both from within and by foreign investors.

15

The War on Poverty Revisited

by Edmund A. Opitz

"Poverty is the natural state of mankind," observes the Reverend Mr. Opitz in this article from the February 1986 Freeman. *He is a member of the staff of The Foundation for Economic Education, a seminar lecturer, book review editor, and author of the book* Religion and Capitalism: Allies, Not Enemies.

In a sense, this essay does not deal directly with the farm problem. But it helps to relate that portion to the more general problem of poverty. And especially helpful is the way in which the author harks back to the wisdom of Adam Smith and the rationale for capitalism. By conquering poverty, capitalism creates the "problem" of poverty. It's much the same with regard to the farm "problem." Only in our affluence do we see abundance to be the problem.

I f we look back over the history of the past two or three thousand years we realize that most people who have ever lived on this planet were desperately poor, not merely poor by our standards—poor by any standards; miserably housed, shabbily clothed, and continually on the verge of starvation, only to go over the edge by the hundreds of thousands during the regularly recurring famines.

Medieval Europe is regarded by many scholars as one of the high points in world civilization. It gave us the great cathedrals, scholastic philosophy, magnificent works of art, literature like Dante's *Divine Comedy*, specimens of craftsmanship that grace our museums, and chivalry. But the Middle Ages in Europe suffered from a number of famines. Between 1201 and 1600 there were seven famines, averaging ten years of famine per century. Coming down to 1709, there was a famine in France that wiped out one million people, five per cent of the population. The last great natural famine in Europe was the Potato Famine in Ireland in the late 1840s, which claimed about one and a half million lives.

But Europe has always been a favored region, more prosperous than the rest of the world, less subject to natural disasters than Asia. There have been starving times in Western civilization, but never were they of the same order of magnitude as the disasters in the Orient. India and China have been especially vulnerable to famines. A famine in China between the years 1876 and 1879 resulted in an estimated 15 million deaths. And within living memory, a famine in China's Hunan Province in 1929 resulted in two million dead. Ten major famines in India between 1860 and 1900 caused the death of close to 15 million people. During the Bengal famine of 1943–44—in and around Calcutta—one and a half million people died of starvation and the epidemics that followed.

I have recited these rather unpleasant facts, not for their own sake, but to emphasize a neglected or overlooked truism: *Poverty is the natural state of mankind.* Poverty is the rule; prosperity is the exception. In most parts of the globe, in most periods of history—including the present—most people most of the time have been or are desperately poor. Prosperity is what the ruling class enjoys. The rich are the superior warriors, the superior hunters, the favorites of the gods, and these wealthy few—it was believed—deserve what they have.

Water runs downhill, fire burns, grass is green, the masses of people are poor. This was the perceived natural order of things, accepted and rarely questioned. Such was the mentality that prevailed throughout most of the world most of the time—until a few centuries ago. Poverty for the multitudes was simply a fact of life. It was a hardship, but being poor was not perceived as deprivation.

The rich were envied, but the envy rarely translated into thoughts of redistributing their wealth. Occasionally something triggered a peasants' revolt or a slave rebellion, but when each of these fizzled out, all ranks went back to "The good old rule/ The simple plan/ That they should take who have the power/ And they should keep who can." Universal poverty was a fact. But poverty was not a problem! The distinction is simple: a fact or situation just is; a fact or situation for which there is perceived to be a solution becomes thereby a problem, and a new mentality is generated.

The Capitalist Alternative

Masses of people, the world over, have now been persuaded that someone or something keeps them poor, and their resentment follows. This fact helps to explain the modern world's hostility toward capitalism. Capitalism is not at all the cause of the poverty of the noncapitalistic nations, but it is the source of their dissatisfaction with their poverty. Capitalism in fact overcomes poverty; but in overcoming poverty capitalism creates the problem of poverty.

There was a breakthrough a few centuries ago, one of those great tidal movements in human affairs resulting in a new mentality and a different way of viewing the human condition. It was the discovery by the people of a few western nations of the complex set of institutions which later came to be called capitalism. The breakthrough might be symbolized by two documents, one penned by Thomas Jefferson setting forth the vision of a nation founded upon a new philosophy, that "all men are created equal," that they are "endowed by their Creator with certain unalienable rights," and that everyone is entitled to equal justice under the law. These axioms form the cornerstone of the free society.

At the same time, on another continent, a man named Smith wrote a great book which explained why the economy need not be centrally planned, directed, and controlled by the government—as it was under the mercantilism of his day. Let the law be vigilant to protect the life, liberty, and property of all—as the Whigs advocated—and the buying habits of freely choosing men and women in the marketplace will provide all the directives needed for the producers to grow and manufacture the things consumers want most. This is the market economy, the backbone of a free society. Under these conditions a free people will multiply their productivity and thus generate their own prosperity,

Capitalism is the name given to the set of institutions which enable free people to produce wealth up to the limit of their time, talents, capacity, and desire; and then to voluntarily exchange the fruits of their labors with others. Capitalism becomes fully operative only when there are institutional guarantees of individual liberty, with laws designed to secure the God-given rights of every person to life, liberty, and property.

The intelligent and ethical way of arranging human action in society, the free society-market economy way of life which we are labeling capitalism, was like a bootstrap by which whole nations of people could and did elevate themselves out of misery, grinding poverty, and periodic starvation. Capitalism tackled poverty using the only means by which poverty can be alleviated, namely, by increased productivity.

Remove every obstacle that hinders the productive and creative energies of men and women and you create an abundance of goods and services, shared by everyone involved according to his contribution to the productive process, as that contribution is judged by the man's peers. This ever-increasing supply of goods and services will move the entire society up the rungs of the ladder of wealth. Some will climb to the top rungs, but even the least well-off on the bottom rungs will experience a level of well-being that would be regarded as affluence in noncapitalistic societies past or present.

Liberty and the Economic Miracle

The results of this new social order were almost miraculous, but there was nothing magical about the way the results were achieved. The results were achieved by people who had the intelligence to understand the requirements of a free and prosperous commonwealth, and who possessed the integrity and character to live by those requirements. We had a significant number of people a couple of centuries ago, who "pledged their lives, their fortunes, and their sacred honor" to establish not simply a new nation, but a nation founded upon new principles.

Capitalism generated a new mentality, a new perception of the human condition. After the experience of capitalism anywhere, people everywhere came to regard prosperity as the rule; poverty as the exception. The fact that we launched a "war on poverty" demonstrates this. No one would contemplate a war on poverty in India or Africa, where need is much more desperate than here. Only in a prosperous nation like our own, where the great war against poverty had already been won—by means of the market economy—would the elimination of the last, lingering remnants of poverty emerge as a political issue. The trouble is that if we employ the wrong remedy to eradicate the remaining pockets of poverty—as we are doing—we may find that we have destroyed prosperity instead, as in the familiar story about killing the goose that laid the golden eggs. Charles Murray's recent book, *Losing Ground*, demonstrates that we have been losing the political war against poverty despite spending hundreds of billions of dollars yearly.

The 18th-century breakthrough I've referred to brought with it a new understanding of how economic goods come into being, the nature of material wealth, and how this new wealth is allocated in differing amounts among all the participants in the productive process. The economic breakthrough was not miraculous; it was preceded by a new vision of how the ancient ideas of liberty, justice, and law should be applied. No longer were these venerable ideas to be the prerogative of the few; equal justice under the law was for everyone; liberty was to be enjoyed by all, and every person had a natural right to the property created by his labor.

For thousands of years the planet was regarded as a static warehouse, containing a fixed amount of wealth, impossible to increase, never enough for everyone. The serf tilling his field grumbled that he had to pay various feudal dues to the lord of the manor, but he was realistic enough to know that even if he kept everything he produced, he'd still go hungry much of the time. He was cursed by low productivity, caused by a faulty understanding of the nature of wealth.

When it is believed that the earth contains only a fixed amount of wealth, the preoccupation is with the allocation of what's already here, which means, invariably, that one man's gain is another's loss.

The new perception that dawned during the 18th century was that new wealth is in a process of continuous creation, in ever-increasing amounts, with more for everyone resulting from each new cycle of production. This new abundance would be distributed—not equally, but equitably—by voluntary exchanges in the marketplace, with each person receiving from his fellows what they think his contribution is worth to them. Each of us benefits in such a voluntary exchange.

This is a paradigm of capitalistic society; peaceful exchanges within the rules, with the rules designed to protect person and property. Each participant in a voluntary exchange is a net gainer, having given up what he wants less to get what he wants more. And as these exchanges multiply every person has a strong inducement to work harder, producing more of the things other people will want from him in exchange. And as each person betters his own circumstances he improves the lives of other people. Production, in a free society, begets production, with more for everyone.

In the pre-capitalistic ages the kings and nobles used their political power to enrich themselves at the expense of the peasants. The serfs who did most of the work were entitled to enjoy only a portion of the goods they produced. Post-capitalistic societies operate in similar fashion. Those who possess political power in welfarist America or socialist Britain or Soviet Russia, exercise the taxing power to deprive productive people of a huge chunk of their earnings. These tax dollars— minus the political costs of effecting these transfers—are then doled out to various "deserving" pressure groups in the private sector.

We witness what Frederic Bastiat might have called a Plunderbund—the law designed to protect life, liberty, and property perverted into an instrument to enrich some by impoverishing others. Albert Jay Nock referred to the law thus perverted as The State—holders of public office in cahoots with factions in the private sector to operate a scam against productive people.

A Private Property Order

Our basic political structures were largely built around the conviction that, "to the producer belongs the fruits of his toil." We were to have a private property order. The Declaration does not mention a right to property, substituting a right to "the pursuit of happiness." We cannot read Jefferson's mind as he wrote the document, but we do know what was in almost everyone else's mind at the time; it was Life, Liberty, and *Property*.

The colonists had migrated out of situations in Europe where they lived on the estate of a master, working mostly for his benefit and only partly for their own. Here in the colonies the idea of freehold property was established. You owned your farm in fee simple, which means that your estate was your very own. You could will it to your descendants, sell it, dispose of it as you wished.

What you produced on your property was yours to keep, or sell, or give away. Now, you owned what your labor created, and you had an enormous incentive to devise labor-saving devices and work harder, longer, and more skillfully because everything you produced was yours. *You* got the added benefit; not some absentee landlord. Wealth creation increased by geometrical progression under these circumstances, with free men and women living under a just system of laws, holding a strict property right in the fruits of their labor.

The American colonists of the 17th and 18th centuries lived in a society whose primary institution was not government, or the press, or business, or the academy; it was the Church. As Alexis de Tocqueville observed of us in the 1830s: "Religion . . . is the first of their political institutions." And it was the colonial churches which labored for the creation of the kind of personal character in men and women which a free society, with its market economy, demands as its basic ingredient.

We are reminded of this need for exemplary character by the late, great economist Wilhelm Roepke who said that the market economy cannot " . . . go on in a moral vacuum . . . . Self-discipline, a sense of justice, honesty, fairness, chivalry, moderation, public spirit, respect for human dignity, firm ethical norms—all of these are things which people must possess before they go to market and compete with each other." And as these early Americans entered the marketplace they practiced the Puritan ethic of work and thrift, believing that thus they served God as co-creators of a new nation, and proved that poverty is not mankind's fate.

The Wealth of the West

The Western World is relatively wealthy because it is relatively capitalistic. The Third World is poor because it shuns capitalism. This is the truth of the matter, obvious to any person who examines the issues impartially. But this truth is overcome by a worldwide ideology which declares that the wealth of the West is the cause of Third World poverty!

President Julius Nyerere of Tanzania voiced this Third World ideology when he wrote: "In one world, as in one state, when I am rich because you are poor, or I am poor because you are rich, the transfer of wealth from the rich to the poor is a matter of right; it is not an appropriate matter for charity." Along the same line, Third World voices tell us that the United States is to blame for the famine in Ethiopia—a country which *exported* its surplus grain and other foodstuffs until the Communists took over.

Third World politicians have a method in their madness: they want things from the West—American dollars, foodstuffs, machinery, and other goods—so they try to convince us that we owe it to them because we are to blame for their plight. This is the Marxist notion that the rich, under capitalism, get richer by making the poor poorer. This ploy would not work except that millions of Americans have also swallowed the Marxist exploitation theory; that those who are better off got that way by making others worse off; that the wealth created by capitalism is the cause of poverty.

Here, for example, are the words from a keynote address given at the World

Council of Churches Assembly held in Vancouver two years ago: "We inhabitants of the industrial nations . . . exploit the majority of the world's population . . . . The demon of profit for the few at the expense of the many, i.e., their impoverishment, has the whole world economic system firmly in its grip." These false and defamatory sentiments are echoed by many academic and ecclesiastical voices, here and abroad.

Americans do consume more than most people elsewhere and it might be interesting to find out why. The answer is simple, to the point of being self-evident: Americans consume more because Americans produce more. Americans produce more, not because we are superior beings, but because our relatively free institutions impose fewer restraints on our productive energies than is the case in other nations, and our private property system guarantees to the producer that he will own the fruits of his toil. Any nation that adopts the free market will be more productive, and thus more prosperous, and in the long run this is the only way to feed the world's hungry.

A False Axiom

The redistributionist policies of our own welfare state, as well as similar international policies which tax Americans in order to subsidize other nations, is based on the false axiom that the wealth of some is the cause of the poverty of others. Something like this *was* true during the pre-capitalistic ages, but capitalism introduced an entirely new ball game in which each one of us prospers to the degree that he contributes to the well-being of other people, as they see it. Walter Lippmann puts it this way: "For the first time in human history men had come upon a way of producing wealth in which the good fortune of others multiplied their own." Freedom in production and exchange does not promise perfection. When people are free, many of their choices may offend us, which means that the free society demands infinite tolerance for each other's foibles. But that's a small price to pay for all the benefits received.

To believe that wealth is the cause of poverty makes as much sense as to assume that health is the cause of disease. And to contend that the remedy for poverty is to soak the rich and give to the poor is as idiotic as believing that the only way to heal the sick is to make the healthy ill. The sick can be made well only as they adopt the sensible regimen of the healthy, and the poor can move out of poverty only as they become more productive. The world's economic problems and other ills will only worsen unless there is a revival of that sound philosophy, which, two centuries ago, gave us the free society and the market economy which I've been labeling capitalism. Education along these lines— replacing bad ideas with better ones—is slow, frustrating, uphill work. But there is no other way.

Meanwhile, we try to live with—while working to correct—the false assumption of people everywhere, that wealth is the cause of poverty. The truth of the matter is that poverty in a nation is caused by the low productivity in that nation. And it is our good fortune that there is a simple recipe for overcoming low productivity while moving in the direction of prosperity. The recipe is: follow the prescriptions of people like Jefferson and Madison; Adam Smith and Bastiat; Mises, Hayek, Roepke, Friedman, and others. The remedy is simple, but simple is not necessarily easy!

Part Four

A Brighter Future

The path to the recovery of freedom—or the formula—is not the same as the tangled route followed on the way into the current mess known as the farm problem. There is no way to coerce others to accept or practice freedom. It is only by his own understanding that anyone achieves a measure of freedom. And there is no blueprint to follow, no single way that any governmental agency or force can impose.

So man's best hope is to offer the rationale for freedom of choice, individual sovereignty, private ownership and control. Signs of innovation and progress may be observed and applauded, examples may be set that others would choose to follow. And in addition to the economic case for freedom, the point must ever be stressed that the right way to treat others is as one would expect to be treated in turn.

16

Freedom for Farmers

by Charles B. Shuman

In this address of December 8, 1969, on the occasion of the fiftieth annual meeting of the American Farm Bureau Federation, Charles Shuman advised American farmers and the American people that it was high time to abandon the programs that had been tried and that had failed—time to rid the United States of welfare state policies and philosophies, time to restore proper respect for law and order.

Mr. Shuman, a farmer, had served as President of the AFBF for fifteen years preceding delivery of this message. He also served as a Trustee of the Foundation for Economic Education for several years. This paper was reprinted in The Freeman, *March 1970.*

We are a nation of frustrated people. The liberals are bitter because their socialist schemes have not produced the results they expected. The intended beneficiaries are unhappy because the promised utopia did not materialize. Black people were promised immediate equality and prosperity. The aged were given increases in social security payments only to find that inflation gobbled up the gains. Union labor was given everything it asked for but the cost of living skyrocketed and some unions have priced their members' services out of the market. Farmers who produce grain and cotton were given price supports and payments but found that these "benefits" were offset by depressed market prices and reduced sales. The poverty program failed to reduce poverty, and socialized medicine for the elderly is a miserable and costly failure. In a desperate effort to make these schemes work the liberal politicians have voted vast increases in power for the Federal government. The excuse was that only the Federal government could provide enough money and move with sufficient speed to break down the barriers that were slowing social and economic reform.

The most recent "national emergency" to be treated to the massive infusion of Federal funds cure is hunger and malnutrition. The White House conference on food, nutrition, and health which was held last week in Washington resulted in new proposals for huge appropriations, and low income is an important factor. The organizer of the conference estimated that there are 30 million hungry people in America but that hunger could be eliminated within three years by appropriating three to five billion dollars per year for food payments out of the Federal treasury.

While there may be 30 million undernourished people in the United States, there are other causes. Much of this so-called hunger is the result of ignorance of proper nutrition, prejudice about food, or unwise dieting practices, and it cannot be cured by food stamps or other spending programs. Like all of its predecessor national emergency programs, the hunger program will probably result in a huge new Federal bureaucracy busily soliciting clients to put on the free food list. Many people will be encouraged to reduce their efforts to help themselves and thus become eligible for food stamps. The ''hunger'' situation may actually worsen rather than improve.

Much of the frustration and unhappiness which has exploded into present-day demonstrations and protests are a direct result of the disappointment of those who expected more than could be delivered by government, and in reality found themselves worse off because of the inflation which destroyed their purchasing power. In difficult times like these it is natural to look for a scapegoat, but I believe that all of us—businessmen, farmers, workers, and professional people—have become obsessed with the notion that we can legislate prosperity for ourselves and—therefore, we must all take the major responsibility for the present trouble. Like Pogo, ''We has found the enemy and he is us.''

Schemes That Failed

If anyone in America has an excuse to be frustrated and bitter, it would be farmers and ranchers. For 40 years, the Congress has experimented with many different schemes to manage production, prices, and marketing of farm products. Almost without exception these schemes have failed, only to be replaced with some new concoction. Even now, the House Agriculture Committee is floundering around trying to find some way to patch up and extend the decrepit and costly Food and Agriculture Act of 1965.

The objective of this legislation was to reduce production and increase prices of feed grain, wheat, and cotton. It has failed in both objectives. The acreage of wheat and feed grains has been cut sharply in the last two years, yet total production has continued to move upwards. Acreage allotments of wheat were cut 13 per cent in 1968 and another 13 per cent in 1969, but the carryover stocks have continued to pile up and the 1.9 billion bushels on hand October 1 is the largest October stock since 1963. Corn and grain sorghum acreage was cut 2 per cent in 1969, but the tonnage harvested was 2 per cent more than the 1968 crop—the carryover is up for the third straight year and now totals 50.2 million tons. The price of wheat fell to the lowest level in 27 years.

The effect of the Act of 1965 on cotton producers is even more discouraging. Despite a government check-off for research, advertising, and promotion, cotton farmers are rapidly losing their market to synthetics—sales are down 5,000 bales per day in two years. Extension of the Act of 1965 could result in completely destroying the cotton industry in the United States. This is overpowering evidence, especially when this sorry record is contrasted with the uncontrolled, unsubsidized, but booming livestock business.

It is obvious that when farmers turned to government, first in 1929 and more definitely in 1933, they took a turn in the wrong direction. Fortunately, Farm Bureau members recognized the mistake several years ago and, almost single-handedly, have prevented the spread of government management to all of agricultural production and marketing. Only about 40 per cent of agricultural production is under government farm programs. Most of the sickness in our industry is in this segment that is government controlled and priced. While Farm Bureau has succeeded in its efforts to block the extension of supply management to livestock, dairy, poultry, and fruits and vegetables, we have not yet succeeded in restoring the government crops to the market place, although most farmers now know that they cannot share equitably in prosperity until this change is made.

"Everyone Else Doing It"

The wrong turn we took in agriculture 40 years ago was motivated by the same needs and desires that have caused other citizens to turn to government for special privileges, subsidies, and protectionist devices. In fact, many farmers have justified their acceptance of controls, subsidies, and price supports with the excuse that "everyone else is doing it." This might be a plausible argument if it could be demonstrated that the government programs have actually benefited farmers. The opposite is true.

Government farm programs have stimulated excess production and have been used to hold farm prices at low levels. One of the major causes of excessive production is the requirement that the support price be announced before the crop is planted. When farmers know the price before planting, they are encouraged to spend more money on fertilizer and other production inputs than they would if the price was uncertain. This one feature of the Food and Agriculture Act of 1965 is probably responsible for much of the increased production that has more than offset the acreage cuts. Yet the cries go up from those who are hooked on payments or who have jobs or warehouses to protect, "It is better than nothing." This is not the alternative, but even if it were, I would challenge this assumption.

While the support prices implemented by Commodity Credit Corporation purchases have at times acted as a floor under the market, they have also acted as a ceiling, and prevented price gains when the supply was short or the demand high. Very seldom have the prices of the government crops risen above the support level. In fact, political management of marketing under the Food and Agriculture Act of 1965 has often depressed prices both in years of abundant production and when the crop was short. When a large crop is in prospect, those in charge of Commodity Credit Corporation marketing tend to panic because they know that it is a political liability to have large quantities of grain piling up in government storage. Under these conditions the domestic market is already overburdened and it is necessary to unload the excess supplies on the world market. During the past summer we have seen a dramatic demonstration of government financed price cutting in the world market for wheat.

International Wheat Agreement

The International Grain Trade Convention (wheat agreement) is an international treaty which was approved by the Senate of the United States in 1968 and which attempted to establish the world price for wheat somewhat above the market price. The ink had hardly dried on the signatures on this treaty before several nations were attempting to find ways to move their huge crops by cutting the price. First one country, then another, including the United States, made sales considerably under the agreed on price. Since the losses incurred in this international price-cutting war were paid by the taxpayers of these wheat producing countries, the cuts in price were far greater than if the losses had come out of the pockets of the individuals who were making the sales.

The international wheat agreement has cost wheat farmers many millions of dollars and should be suspended immediately. If the other nations party to the agreement will not agree to a suspension, the United States should announce that it will not be bound by the terms of this now discredited scrap of paper.

It may seem strange but a similar downward pressure on markets is exerted by the Commodity Credit Corporation in a short crop year. Government supply managers also tend to panic in a short crop season especially if the housewives begin to picket the retail stores to complain about high retail food prices. The farmers and ranchers of America were given a painful demonstration of this panic about three years ago when Secretary of Agriculture Orville Freeman dumped hundreds of millions of bushels of grain on the market to hold feed prices down in an effort to stimulate livestock feeding. During recent months the Commodity Credit Corporation has been moving substantial quantities of wheat into the feed grain market.

When Congress passed the Food and Agriculture Act of 1965, it included provision for making direct payments to farmers. This action in itself was an admission that the net effect of government-managed production, pricing, and marketing was to reduce the prices to farmers. These direct payments have only been a partial offset to the market price losses sustained under this legislation. Approximately 23 per cent of net farm income is now represented by these payments and cotton farmers look to these payments for about 40 per cent of their gross receipts from cotton lint.

Further Payments No Help in Getting "Unhooked"

Causing farmers to be dependent on Congressional appropriations for so much of their income is a sorry state of affairs and one which cannot be continued if there is to be a good future for farmers. Consumers and taxpayers look upon these payments in the same light as they look upon welfare payments to the poverty stricken. This means that limitations on the amount paid to any one producer will be imposed and eventually Agricultural Stabilization and Conservation "case workers" will supervise the spending of these "welfare" checks. Many farmers are hooked on payments because the price in the market has been depressed to such a low level that their only hope of covering production expenses is to add the payments to the market price. However, the solution is not to continue payments. The only sensible approach is to find a way to get unhooked.

Getting unhooked from farm programs will be a costly operation because the distortions and imagined advantages of the programs have been capitalized into land values and machinery.

Three Steps to Decontrol

There are three essentials that must be adhered to in any program to change directions. First, the unsuccessful attempts to control production by government allotments and quotas must be terminated. Acreage controls have been worse than useless—they have actually stimulated surplus production. Second, price supports have acted as a ceiling to prevent price increases and must be phased out or keyed to market prices if farmers are to share in the prosperity of our competitive enterprise economy. Third, welfare type direct payments in lieu of competitive prices must be phased out.

Making the transition from the present program to a market price agriculture should not be too difficult once the Congress has agreed on the objective of phasing out government supply management in agriculture.

The temptation for farmers to seek an "easy" way to develop market power remains, even though Federal control of production and pricing have proven unsuccessful. Those who would "let the government do it" favor nationwide marketing orders, Federal marketing boards, or other government supervised and managed marketing and bargaining. Government has a proper and important role in the marketing system; however this role is not to supervise marketing or to participate in the price-making process. Government should act as a referee to establish rules and to protect consumers against conspiracies to set price, or other monopolistic practices.

Experience in other countries with government marketing boards and other devices to control the marketing of farm products have proven to be ineffective and unsatisfactory from the farmers' standpoint. Here again, political appointees who administer the programs must please the majority of voters—the 95 per cent who are consumers. It is inevitable that any government price management will result in holding prices down to please this big consumer majority. The egg marketing board in the United Kingdom was recently abandoned because it had stimulated surplus production, depressed prices, reduced the quality, and increased the retail cost of eggs. If the labor-socialist government of the United Kingdom, which is dedicated to a managed economy, cannot control the egg market, who can say that our government can manage the marketing of any agricultural commodity successfully?

Congress Must Control Spending

Nineteen-seventy will perhaps be one of the most crucial election years in history. The nation is in need of a change in direction. That change can come if the new Congress is willing to accept its responsibility to control Federal spending. Government, fiscal, and monetary policies must be stabilized and the budget brought into balance. Irresponsibility in high public office invites the same attitude by the people. Much of the bitterness and frustration which is evidenced in the demonstrations and riots is in part a by-product of government fiscal irresponsibility. Extravagant promises of instant prosperity and total security could not be fulfilled, and so the disillusioned protested.

Much of the present discontent probably should be charged up to the rapidly escalating inflation which is boosting prices and destroying the value of savings. Inflation is caused by huge government spending programs to satisfy the demands of the citizens for ever-increasing government benefits—the "something for nothing" idea. The costly war in Vietnam has generated inflation but so too have the multi-billion-dollar domestic spending programs, such as urban renewal, poverty, and farm subsidies.

Centuries ago, Pericles said: "Happiness is freedom and freedom is courage." In our search for the good life we have been concentrating on material comforts while neglecting more fundamental values. True happiness cannot be purchased, it cannot be found in material comforts alone.

Undoubtedly, much of the current turmoil is the result of the frustration experienced by many people when they find that money and things have not brought happiness. It is also probable that increasing restrictions on individual freedom are being felt but not always identified. Ever higher property taxes, sales taxes, income taxes, and surtaxes are required to pay for planned society schemes, and this reduces the individual's freedom to spend his income.

Furthermore, the welfare state breeds countless rules and regulations as thousands of new laws are passed each year. Big government and individual freedom are not compatible.

Money, luxury goods, leisure time, security from the cradle to the grave—all these are valued by many people but they alone do not bring happiness. What we need in America is a big dose of courage: courage to take a position on controversial issues; courage to reject compromise between good and evil; courage to take a stand on moral issues; courage to refuse to be "bought" by government payments or private bribes; courage to accept risk as the price for opportunity.

Produce for the Market, Not for Government Storage

Up to now, this has been a rather doleful recital of the sad state of affairs in the United States generally, and particularly in agriculture. If we stopped here in our analysis, the conclusion could be drawn that the future is bleak, but I am optimistic. I believe that the next few years will bring a change in direction, a change in the attitude of people toward government and new hope for farmers as they seek to produce for consumer markets rather than government storage.

The time for a change is long past due. It is time to rid the United States of welfare state policies and philosophies. Time to return government to its proper role of providing a healthy economic climate for private enterprise rather than attempting to guarantee security from the cradle to the grave. Time to recognize the failure of the wild spending "new economics" theories and to re-establish government fiscal responsibility by balancing the budget. Time to abandon government policies that force farm families to depend upon welfare type subsidy payments for their income. Time to re-establish a free market agriculture with income derived from profits. Time to restore proper respect for law and order.

17

A Nongovernmental Farm Program

by Paul Roy

Contract farming may not be the only answer to the farm problem. But it is an interesting alternative to the "easy solution" of pumping additional billions of taxpayer funds into the farm program. This article is from the June 1959 Freeman. The contract farming described by Dr. Roy, Agricultural Economist at Louisiana State University, involves arrangements between farmers and farm supply companies to jointly produce broilers, hogs, beef cattle, eggs, canning crops, and other commodities without Federal funding. There is a better way!

Many persons have followed the path of least resistance to the conclusion that the only solution to American agricultural problems is for the federal government to pour billions into the farm program. But I cannot agree that our only salvation rests in Washington. I doubt that the Congress or any federal agency is capable of enacting and administering a comprehensive farm program with justice or equity. Our agriculture is too diversified for that, our farms varying in size and capitalization, with wide dispersions in income that are aggravated rather than corrected by government payments to farmers.

We have agricultural resources committed to wheat, corn, cotton, rice, and other crops, with yields vastly in excess of the quantity which can be moved at the support price. This hurts domestic industries which must buy in this price-supported market. It also hurts our prospects in foreign markets, where we hold a price umbrella over competitors, thus increasing any advantage they might otherwise have had.

Yet, while economists and others have been busy devising and trying to enforce unworkable programs, a kind of technological revolution has been happening in many lines of farming—especially livestock and poultry. This went largely unnoticed in the American press until a year ago. The United States Department of Agriculture and many of the agricultural colleges failed to realize the extent and importance of this potential change in farming patterns.

The change involves economic integration, more popularly called contract farming. However, this contract is not between the government and the farmer; it is an economic arrangement between businessmen and farmers. The businessmen supply all or part of the credit and the production supplies and assure a market for the produce. The farmer, in turn, supplies as many resources as he can, including all or part of the productive labor. In exchange, the farmer gets a guaranteed return for his labor plus a share of profits above a certain level.

Broiler Growers on Contract

Contract farming had its real beginning in the broiler industry where it attained a high degree of perfection and performance. The system is now spreading to hogs, beef cattle, table eggs, hatching eggs, canning crops, and to many other farm enterprises, except those supported by the government. The crops subject to government price support account for less and less of the national agricultural income. For example, poultry income is now in first place in Georgia and Alabama, and ranks high in the other southern states of Arkansas, Louisiana, Mississippi, South Carolina, North Carolina, and Texas. Economic integration started here because cotton was being price-and-acreage-controlled out of its markets; the price support program indirectly led to economic integration.

This contract farming in broilers, for example, has been so successful that broiler meat consumption has gained considerably on competing meats such as beef, veal, and pork. Broiler prices in retail food stores are lower than during the Depression days. Economists say the results of economic integration in hogs and table eggs could be just as outstanding. Some persons claim that broiler growers on contract work for "starvation" wages, but the facts refute them. Recent research by Southern land-grant colleges shows that net labor returns to broiler growers on contract averaged $1.10 per hour.

The farmer has always faced the uncertainties of weather, animal and insect pests, diseases, and income and price fluctuations; and he is fully justified in trying to reduce or eliminate such hazards. But the result, when he has turned to the government for help, has been the added aggravation of long debates, red-tape, and a huge bureaucracy. Far better that farmers work out satisfactory production, marketing, and income arrangements with businessmen who are in business to supply a market rather than to fill a government warehouse.

Advantages of Integration

What are the advantages of economic integration in agriculture? (1) It does not require government regulation or subsidy because it is a self-adjusting mechanism through the market place. (2) It spreads risks, including that of price fluctuation, among the people who do the integrating. (3) It is based on and builds respect for the personal integrity and the private property rights of all parties involved—farmer, businessman, consumer. (4) It shifts or absorbs within its own organization some of the costs of research, teaching, and demonstration. (5) It has no monopoly advantage or power because it relies on economic and technological efficiency in its operations and is not a device for market control.

What is the moral taught us by agricultural economic integration? It is simple:

Stop interfering; leave people to their own resources and ingenuity, free to attempt something new, free to produce and trade voluntarily to their mutual advantage. In whatever you do—farming, teaching, manufacturing—aim for one thing: produce and offer the goods and services people want and can afford to pay for.

Woe to those who produce for a warehouse or cave or mothball fleet far removed from the exacting needs of the market, those who teach the tempting but false philosophy of something-for-nothing, those who hide their inefficiencies behind special privileges, subsidies, and protective trade barriers. Any possible short-run gains from such tactics are strictly illusory, for they are at the expense of others, harmful to society, and in the long run destructive of the very ones who seek them. While the pains of adjustment to the market are sometimes acute, they are preferable to the chronic and eventually incurable disease of subsidy and control.

18

The New Agricultural Revolution

by George B. Mueller

Mr. Mueller of upstate New York operates a family farm specializing in dairy and cash crops. In this article from the May 1972 Freeman, *he explains that farmers then were investing twice as much as the industry average in capital and tools per man. In other words, farming is big business, there has been an agricultural revolution, and the conventional wisdom about the hardships suffered on the family farm no longer necessarily apply. The winds of change are blowing, and the key to success is competition.*

Every American school boy and girl is familiar with the agricultural revolution. It was this revolution that enabled American workers to leave the farm and build a great nation. The modern techniques and tools used on our present-day, family-operated, commercial farms are the envy of the world. Even Premier Khrushchev came over to take a first-hand look at our tremendous agricultural productivity. Our family farms, bigger and more efficient than ever, are putting food on the typical American's table for less than 17 per cent of his wages. Certainly, if there ever was a success story, it is America's family farm.

As farmers, we are presently investing twice the amount industry averages in capital tools per man. Because of this heavy capital investment, and the fact that most farmers still put in a full day of productive work, our American farm products remain competitive in world markets. In contrast, each year that passes, we see more and more of our industries failing to meet competition abroad. The shelves in our stores are increasingly stocked with products "Made in Japan" and elsewhere.

In spite of nearly nine billion dollars of farm products exported last year (1971), the United States experienced a minus balance of trade for the first time in

83 years. To make matters worse, dock worker strikes have seriously curbed agricultural feedgrain exports, threatening a permanent loss of markets that took years to develop. Thus, agriculture, one of our few industries still able to compete, has been partially shut off from world markets. Our family-based agriculture, the strongest in the world, has a tremendous ability to compete if only permitted to do so.

"The Farm Problem"

Agriculture is over-crowded, as are most other businesses in the United States. We have too many drug stores, too many hardware stores, too many grocery stores, too many insurance salesmen, too many barber shops, and so on. This is the American way. Businessmen are supposed to be free to enter any field of production and trade in which they think they can make a profit. The result is keen competition in most businesses. The consumer benefits from competition by getting better service and lower prices. Competition also has resulted in numerous business failures. The typical business earns a slim profit, if any. Only the best managed firms (those that serve the consumer best), reap a substantial profit. Such is the nature of our cherished system of competitive enterprise.

The agricultural business is especially crowded because it was the original and only way of life for many Americans. The movement of workers out of agriculture has not been rapid enough to prevent this over-crowding. Farming generally is a wholesome, healthy, and satisfying work, and many people are willing to accept a lower standard of living rather than give up such a way of life. Farming, because of its appeal, will always be crowded, and profit margins for the "average" farmer will always be low. Only the well-managed farm, operated with a judicious amount of modern tools and the latest know-how, will yield a good profit. This is as it should be, for this type of farm operation is serving the consumer best.

Time and again we hear dire predictions of the take-over of farming by corporations. It is true that the family farm has changed and tends to look more like a factory every day. My neighbor used to be one of the largest poultry farmers in the county with 3,000 layers—and quite successful. But progress has left him behind. Those in the vicinity who intend to stay with chickens are building 500-foot-long houses to hold 43,000 birds in wire cages, wall-to-wall. There are still family-owned and -operated farms, but they are large and efficient. Likewise, the dairy farms of 30 years ago with 12 cows are now either out of business or have grown much larger. They, too, are still family-owned and -operated. The only corporate agriculture in my county consists of a few acres of vineyards owned by a winery. The United States Department of Agriculture reports that corporations account for only 1 per cent of our farms, 7 per cent of our farm land and 8 per cent of our agricultural production. A closer look reveals that ninety per cent of these are actually family farms that have incorporated to ease the transfer to the next generation. It is apparent that the family farm that has mechanized and is under the skillful management of its owner is still very competitive. Corporations, with their high fixed costs, have found it almost impossible to compete with the American family farm.

I think we do not have a "farm problem." In fact, agriculture, because of the private research by feed, seed, building supply, chemical, machinery, and fertilizer companies, has kept up with modern methods as well as has any U.S. industry. The development of hybrid seed corn is an excellent example of how private researchers, competing for a profit, benefit all of us—especially the consumer. The research by Land Grant Colleges and by the U.S.D.A. has supplemented and stimulated this private research. Agri-business salesmen, farm catalogs, advertising folders, and numerous farm publications, in addition to government-sponsored agricultural extension service (county agents), have made this valuable research available to all American farmers—big and small. Use of this modern knowledge has made the American family farm the most efficient in the world. Rather than looking upon agriculture as a serious problem, we should consider it our biggest success story.

The Winds of Change

A fundamental change is taking place in the thinking of the American farmer. We have long been singled out by politicians as a group of people to be pitied. Farm publications keep telling us how much we suffer. Our farm leaders are especially sympathetic to our "sad" plight and pledge all sorts of programs to bring us aid. We farmers have heard this so long and so often that we are beginning to believe it.

The independent, self-reliant, self-thinking farmer is wavering. So often told that we must cooperate with others and "set our own price," we are beginning to move in this direction. The appeal of collective bargaining is gaining momentum among farm people. Farm editors and farm leaders would not dare suggest that competitors in any other business get together to set prices; yet, they boldly advocate a monopoly control over supply by farmers, using such terms as "disciplined marketing" or "supply management." When examined closely, their object is a monopoly control over the total supply. The result is presumed to be higher prices and returns for the farmer at the expense of the consumer. But let us look at how this will affect the family farm.

The family farm is dominant in America today because it is a *strong competitor*. It is dominant because of its ability to survive in periods of low prices. The family farmer can let the hired man go and work harder himself in periods of low prices. The farmer's wife can even take a job in town in order to help save the farm. These are options not available to the larger, more heavily capitalized corporate farms.

Interestingly enough, many of the farmers working the hardest for collective bargaining—and the security that the higher and more stable prices will bring— are the large operators. Through careful management and hard work, they have built large efficient enterprises which they now wish to protect. In periods of high prices, they prosper. But low prices put the large farms to the test, causing many to fail. Fluctuating farm prices thus tend to even the score, so that the little fellow has an opportunity to compete. What will happen to the small family farm when collective bargaining assures stable high prices for the large farmer? Won't this be the opening corporations are looking for and won't they come pouring into agriculture once we assure a higher profit margin?

To limit "over-production" when bargaining achieves a better price for farmers, there will have to be some kind of a quota system. Just as laborers wait in line to work on union jobs, so shall young farmers wait in line to farm. In good growing years we will be forced to let a portion of the crop rot to insure higher prices from the consumer. It will be an entirely new ball game for the self-reliant, independent, competitive farmer. But he will adjust, once he tastes the fruits of collective action.

As time goes on, I anticipate that these quotas will be purchased by the larger growers; and the larger growers will merge and form even larger corporations. Once we establish "rights" as to who can farm and how much, we are opening the door to big business in farming. Just as truckers' "rights" are soon purchased by the larger trucking firms, the farmers' "rights" will also flow toward where the money is. By turning to collective bargaining, we may be dooming the family farm.

We already have legislation to prevent buyers from discriminating against us when we sell cooperatively—The Agricultural Fair Practice Act. The National Agricultural Marketing and Bargaining Act (Sisk Bill) is about to be passed in Congress. It would force the buyer of farm products to negotiate in good faith with his regular suppliers and prevent him from buying from other sources during these negotiations. The next logical legislative step will be a requirement for compulsory arbitration if negotiations fail. Along with this will have to come a limit on entry and quotas for all existing farmers.

In summary, we are witnessing in a few short years the coming of a monopolistic type of collective bargaining for agriculture. Farmers are accomplishing this through strong and efficient lobbies in Washington. Farmers may soon have the collective bargaining powers that it took labor a century of bloodshed to obtain. Even the U.S.D.A., after 35 years of all sorts of farm programs that have failed, now suggests that we try farm bargaining. The collective bargaining juggernaut is rolling in high gear and is on a collision course with the family farm. There is definitely an agricultural revolution in progress.

The Consumer Is Still King

The first principle of business is that the customer is king. To prosper over a period of years, a business must serve the customer well. Now, as farmers, we find ourselves looking at our customers as adversaries from whom we should demand better prices rather than earn them. Like many unionized wage earners in our society, we foolishly believe we can raise our standard of living by demanding more for doing less.

The time has come for the American consumer to remind the farmer that he is a *businessman*, expected to compete as he produces the food and fiber that our nation needs. Farmers are no more justified in getting together to manipulate prices than are oil companies, or auto companies, or drug companies, or any other business competitors. It is time to remind the farmer that competition is still the foundation of free enterprise. True, farmers have more votes and, therefore, more power in Washington than have other businesses. But does this justify a war against consumers? The consumer, if alerted, has more power—economic or political—than any conceivable combination of producers. Perhaps it is time for consumers to take a hand in steering a course for agriculture.

19

Lasers, Harobeds, and World Hunger

by Howard Baetjer Jr.

Howard Baetjer, now on the staff at FEE, was a graduate student in political science at Boston College in 1983 when this article first appeared in a campus paper and was reprinted in The Freeman *in August of that year. He drew upon his experiences as a summer field hand on an alfalfa ranch to show how inventions and machines and technological progress would do far more to solve the problems of hunger than all the schemes of redistribution governments could devise.*

What do lasers have to do with world hunger? They help decrease it, that's what. Of course it is a complex story, though it all transpired in a remarkably short time. Development of the laser won a Nobel Prize in 1962, and less than twenty years later lasers were being used to level fields in the parched Humboldt River Valley of Nevada (among other places), to improve irrigation. When a field 1200 ft. long drops off at the rate of .21 ft. in every hundred, given the kind of soil they have in the Humboldt Valley, water released into the field at the high end will slide out just as evenly as can be and soak into the entire field in precisely the same amount all over.

The laser allows the rancher to get the fields absolutely flat, and dropping off at exactly the right rate. At one end of the field an instrument is set up and adjusted so that it emits a plane of laser light at exactly the right angle. This light is read by a sensor attached to a huge machine with a scraping blade and a reservoir of topsoil. When the ground rises up, the sensor tells the blade to shave the area down some; when the ground drops off, it tells the machine to dump some soil.

Once a field has been laser-planed, if the irrigator lets in the right amount of water at the right rate, irrigation will be perfectly even, and the alfalfa growing

120

there will soak up the water and the hot Nevada sun, and grow up so thick and so fast that it looks like something out of Walt Disney Productions. And it will grow like that over every square foot of the field: all the way to all the edges, with no dry spots and no muddy areas the way there always used to be. It is an amazing thing, I assure you—I have cut both kinds of fields.

The importance of all this to world hunger is that alfalfa is terrific feed for livestock. By making alfalfa production more efficient, laser technology provides us a means of feeding more livestock, one source of food for the hungry of the world. Those fields produce an average of 37 and a half 135-pound bales per acre, three times a summer. That's 15,187.5 pounds of hay per acre.

When you figure that a healthy cow eats about 24 pounds of hay a day, that means each acre of those fields produces enough hay in a summer to feed a cow for 633 days, or a herd of 21 cows for a month. An acre, bear in mind, is smaller than a football field. A standard 40-acre field (almost all of which I could cut myself in a single ten-hour day) would yield enough hay to feed 70 cows for a year. That's a whole lot of milk and cheese and butter. The point is that if we could get more areas of the world producing the way the Humboldt River Valley does, the world hunger problem would start to disappear.

The Inadequacy of Redistribution

I use this little illustration from my own experience by way of disagreement with my college's World Hunger Committee, and similar groups which advocate redistribution as a solution to the world's dreadful problem of want. In our campus cafeteria there is a poster put up by the World Hunger Committee, which gives some figures about production, consumption, and hunger in different parts of the world. It points out that we in the United States consume far more per person than people in other nations and concludes with this: ''Redistribution is necessary for the future.''

Though the World Hunger Committee is to be applauded for its concern and efforts to bring the problem to our attention, their poster does not point out the reason for the problem, and the solution it proposes is utterly inadequate and ill-advised. Hunger is not a distribution problem, and redistribution cannot possibly solve it. Hunger is a production problem; the only thing that can solve it is the political and economic change that will allow production to occur.

Redistribution as a ''solution'' to the problem of hunger is apparently premised on the assumption that there is only a certain amount to go around. Reallocating what food there is now in the world might, under ideal circumstances, alleviate the hunger problem for a while. It could never do away with it. Even now there is not enough to go around with any sort of bounty, and in any case the population of the world is growing. Relying on redistribution would mean resigning ourselves to progressively less and less for each as ''the world's goods'' were split up among more and more. This is an unnecessarily despairing response to the problem, for it is not true that ''there is only a certain amount to go around.''

The Productive Potential

Potentially, there is plenty to go around. There are many areas of the world which could be supplying food at tremendously greater rates than currently. Land presently in cultivation could be made to produce more; the crops grown there could be improved or replaced with others more suited to a given soil or climate; land presently out of cultivation could be made productive with irrigation, drainage, fertilizers, and the like; planting and harvesting methods could be improved; transportation of crops to markets could be improved; refrigeration could reduce spoilage, and so on. The potential to improve production is, if not boundless, limited only by people's ingenuity, which has throughout history produced tremendous gains wherever it has been left free to work its miracles.

Consider the case of the ranch in Nevada. One hundred years ago, maybe much less, a lot of the land now bursting with alfalfa was desert, considered inarable. Nothing much grew there but sagebrush, and the Humboldt River flowed by at a distance, gradually evaporating and finally drying up completely in one of those amazingly barren Nevada salt basins. How did that land come to be such a cornucopia?

• Labor, for one thing. The first irrigation ditches were probably dug with picks and shovels, the first fields smoothed out as well as possible by hand, the ranchers filling in the low spots as well as they could by eye. Machines do most of the physical work now, but there is still a whole lot of labor in maintaining them, driving them, building fences, and the like.

• Tools, for another: picks, shovels and hoes were the staples at first, I suppose, and then mule-drawn plows and harrows, rudimentary surveying gear to help smooth out the fields, scythes for the harvesting and so on. Better techniques and materials contributed, too: fertilizers, irrigation by sections (with levees to keep the water level more even), and so on.

As time went by, the tools were improved, and for the same amount of labor the amount that could be produced increased steadily. With the internal combustion engine there came self-powered machines for digging the irrigation ditches, pulling the plows and hay wagons, and running the balers. With modern chemistry there came better fertilizers; biologists developed better strains of alfalfa; metallurgists provided cutting blades that kept an edge longer. With each step the same land and labor produced more hay.

Finally—most recently, I should say, for who knows what next year will bring—there came laser planes and harobeds (that's *Deborah* backwards, named after the wife of the man who invented them): truck-like machines which, with a scoop and a system of conveyors and platforms, pick up and arrange seventy bales at a time, carry them to the stack lot, and put them down neatly (if the driver is skillful!), to wait for the big flatbeds that will take them away to markets in four or five states. The newest harobeds at the ranch where I work have a little computer that keeps track of the bales and lays them together in an interlocking fashion that stacks better than was possible previously, reducing moisture loss. Step by step, improvement by improvement, machine by machine, the desert bloomed and burgeoned forth with ever greater quantities of hay.

This same kind of process can go on, according to the necessities of each climate and location, all over the world. Lands that are poor can become rich. People who now lean over all day planting rice shoot by shoot can go to other productive endeavors, leaving behind them ever fewer others, who will grow ever more rice with ever better machines, fertilizers and techniques. As the desert bloomed, so can the swamplands, the hillsides, and the jungles (not to mention the good lands now way below potential) as long as labor and ever better tools are applied to them.

The Heart of the Problem

From this point of view, we can begin to see why there are so many hungry people in the world. Certainly there is no lack of labor—in the poorest countries everyone works in every available way to try to make ends meet. The problem lies with the productivity of that labor. The backbreaking labor of twenty men working with trowels could not plant in a day what a single one of them could plant in the same time on a modern planter. The same twenty men with sickles could not harvest in a day the forty acres of alfalfa I can cut, sitting comfortably in the air-conditioned cab of a Sperry-New Holland "swather." Until they have better tools, the poor areas of the world will stay poor.

And this brings us to the heart of the matter. In order to have good tools, particularly the complex machinery that can bring about plenty, there must be a highly complex and efficient economic system in which production and maintenance of such tools is possible. There must be room for innovation, so that new, more efficient ideas may be put into practice. There must be hard work, so that plans are thoughtfully made and thoroughly executed. There must be efficient allocation of resources. There must be risk-taking, for in an uncertain world one cannot know what tools will work well and therefore be in demand. Inefficient or obsolete processes and means of production must disappear, to make room for the newer and better. Above all, there must be the accumulation of capital: people must save money in large quantities, so that the funds will be available to support the complex and time-consuming process of machine-building.

This means, in turn, that there must be economic freedom. What must be avoided above all are the repressive economic policies that grow out of a redistributive approach to society. People cannot innovate by command, or when burdened by regulation. There is no incentive to work hard when the fruits of one's labor are taken from him (presumably to be "redistributed"). There can be no efficient resource allocation where prices cannot vary according to the laws of supply and demand. There will be no risk-taking if people are not allowed to realize the rewards of taking them. Inefficient and obsolete practices will not give way to newer and better when they are protected by government. And there will be no capital accumulation—the lifeblood of production—when savings are heavily taxed, when profits are taken away, when inheritance is outlawed. The redistributive ethos, which inhibits production at every step, could reasonably be said to be the fundamental reason why hunger persists in the world so long after the technical means of eradicating it have been available.

The Solution

If the tools necessary to feed the world are going to come into existence, the world must take a big political step forward. Government intervention in the economy must be abandoned. People must be left free to produce, and they must be allowed to have the benefit of their productivity. They must be allowed to own the means of production, to accumulate fortunes, and to trade freely with one another, without restraint by some authority which purports to know what is good for them better than they themselves.

Ultimately, the solution to the problem of world hunger lies in free enterprise, in the profit and loss system, in the private property order—in *capitalism*. Only in this kind of economic freedom are the marvelous creative abilities of human beings released. Redistribution is impossible without prior production. Redistribution could never have turned that Nevada desert green. But with swathers and balers and harobeds, with tractors and irrigation ditches and laser-planes—with the fruits of enterprise and accumulated capital, in short—the desert blooms. Redistribution is not necessary for the future; capitalism is.

20

Agriculture and the Survival of Private Enterprise

by Ed Grady

"Private enterprise can, and shall, survive in America," testifies Mr. Grady. And so he has testified for more than 30 years professionally telling the story of freedom. He was manager of the information division of the Minnesota Farm Bureau Federation when this essay appeared in the August 1979 issue of The Freeman. *Read especially the powerful appeal in the concluding two paragraphs of the essay.*

O ne of the most compelling problems we face, as a nation and as a people, is embodied in the question, "Can private enterprise survive in America?"

And my answer to that question is a qualified one: "Yes, private enterprise can, and shall, survive in America . . . providing":

- providing that as Americans we quit taking it for granted
- providing we understand what makes our system tick
- providing we learn how to make both an emotional and intellectual sale in behalf of freedom
- providing we care enough to make the good fight.

And what is agriculture's role in the survival of free enterprise in America? Simply put, it is to demonstrate our ability, and our willingness, to measure up to the test provided by each of these provisos. This we are determined, and dedicated, to do.

If we demonstrate as much integrity in organizing support for freedom as its opponents have demonstrated in attacking it, then no question but that we shall win the battle.

If there is one lesson that history tells us again and again it is that concentration of power and authority in "big government" is, eventually and certainly, followed by the loss of personal freedom. And let us never forget that no man's future is safe in the hands of a political philosophy that is willing to buy today's popularity with tomorrow's agony.

Economic freedom is the foundation of political freedom. The two are inseparable.

Make no mistake about it; every time we transfer responsibility and power to a central government, we transfer responsibility and power away from the people.

All of us—the businessman on Main Street and the businessman on the farm included—need a basic understanding of what it is that makes private competitive enterprise go.

The mainsprings of the system are four in number:

(a) Most property privately owned;
(b) Most property privately managed;
(c) Most property operated for a profit, not necessarily at a profit; and
(d) All this under circumstances in which competition prevails.

All production—all civilization, in fact—rests on a recognition of and respect for property rights. A private enterprise system is impossible without security of property; it is possible only within a framework of law and order and morality.

When a man's property rights are protected, he is able to retain and enjoy in peace the fruits of his labor. This security is his main incentive, if not his only incentive, to labor creatively. If anyone were free to confiscate what the farmer had sown, fertilized, cultivated and raised, he would no longer have any incentive to sow or to reap.

Profit is the life blood of a free economy. The opportunity to make a profit (or the opposite, the discipline of possible loss) is the invisible hand, as it were, that guides production and distribution. And in guiding the economy to the satisfaction of society's needs, the profit system does what no central authority is capable of doing as well—even granting that the authority might be staffed by the most brilliant planners and the best able managers among us.

It is said at times that many are willing to trade freedom for security. Even if they were to receive that for which they traded, it would be a bad bargain. But the sad and frightening fact is that when a people seek to obtain security by turning over power and responsibility to government, they lose both freedom and security.

What we must recognize, of course, is that there simply is no real security in any form of society that rests upon centralized political and economic control.

Life in such societies is grim and drab and desperate. The opportunity of the individual to better himself is hamstrung by restrictions and frustrations and limitations which stifle initiative and suffocate progress. The individual in this kind of situation becomes a mere cog in a rusty, creaking, poorly-functioning machine.

Our form of society is being battered today by the most subtle and most dangerous threat possible—the destruction of the competitive market system. It is most subtle and most dangerous because it always is done with the avowed purpose of benefiting or protecting some segment of our population.

A Flexible Price System

In our economy, it is a flexible price system that serves as the balance wheel for the whole structure. The price system determines how much of any product we should produce; it adjusts consumption to use what is produced; and it guides the flow of investment to insure the production of what is needed.

Now, if we don't permit the price system to perform these functions, we strike deep into the very lifeline, at the very heart, of our competitive economic system. And if the capacity of the price system to perform its function is destroyed, there remains only one alternative: assign the authority to fix prices to government or, put another way, to political management.

Political management of our price system is inevitably inefficient, cumbersome, backward-looking and costly. Even though the appointed fixers were all-intelligent supermen, it would be impossible for them to operate effectively in a situation in which every decision is affected by political considerations and political pressures. Personal ambitions and bureaucratic policies become major factors influencing every decision.

For a physician, the least profitable patient is a dead one. The next least profitable is the well one. The gold mine is the patient who continues sick, or continues to think himself sick. The nobility of the medical profession is the fact that few of us have ever had an encounter with doctors who exploit this obvious truth.

But not always so with politicians. Many of them parade as physicians to doctor the economic ills of their constituents. Our need for protection from exploitation in this instance is less obvious—but far more necessary.

Government farm policy dating back some 40 years has been so long on promises and so lean on performance because it is borrowed from the strategy and tactics of the coercive society and its centrally-directed and centrally-controlled economy. It serves well neither producers nor consumers.

Thus the all-consuming importance of choices, and how it is that one of our continuing challenges is to discover in advance the eventual consequences of the choices we are called upon to make. This is an absolute prerequisite not only of successful self-government but essential also to the survival of private enterprise.

The discussion over the years with regard to compensatory payments (target prices, in the current government farm program glossary) illustrates well what it is one or another choice involves.

Basically, what is wrong with the payment approach?

It is not, as advocates even today claim, a device to control production; it is a scheme to control farmers. Nor is it, as some contend, a plan to establish a free market; it is a proposal to wreck markets. Simply put, it provides an engraved invitation for politically-determined limitations on the farm incomes of individual producers—and it's ideally suited to implement the concept of rationing the right to earn on the basis of the politics of equal shares. Instead of easing the cost-price squeeze which plagues farmers in Minnesota and throughout the country, it makes matters worse.

Some years ago, the late Aneurin Bevan and his British Labor Party colleagues published in a pamphlet the basic tenets of their political philosophy. If there is one phrase more than any other that appears time and again in this document, it is the term "fair shares."

Reduced to its most common denominator, fair shares is nothing more and nothing less than a political device for leveling and putting a ceiling on opportunity. This is not the American way; this is the other way!

A moment's reflection on the fair-shares doctrine should make us aware that it is time for individual citizens to reaffirm their faith in capitalism, American style.

Curbing the Intervention

Authoritarian liberals delude themselves into believing they are champions of liberty while favoring creeping coercion as long as they can be authors of the coercion. While they are trying to cure injustice by piling on more government, they lose sight of the fact that all the great struggles for freedom have been directed against the overblown force of government.

There isn't a one of us—in town or in the country—who isn't a target of the propaganda campaign being waged by what I call the "cult of the positive." The conviction of people who make up this breed is that you don't have a "positive" program for solving problems unless you have a program that calls for government intervention, or government involvement—preferably national— and the more widespread the better. These economic meddlers and political peddlers are determined to be positive—even if it means being positively wrong.

All of which causes me to suggest that if you really know what you're for, you won't hesitate to be against anything that is inconsistent with it. If you're for good, solid, juicy crunchy apples, you just have to be against worms. The chaos and confusion arises when people don't know what they're for.

So if you're for the private competitive enterprise system, it won't disturb you to oppose proposals that would wreck the market system. If you're for the voluntary method of solving problems, you'll not hesitate to fight efforts to substitute compulsion or coercion. And if you're for individual responsibility, freedom and opportunity, you'll forthrightly and vigorously oppose anything inconsistent with this fundamental concept.

That's the logic, and the rationale, of liberty.

Dr. Norman Vincent Peale didn't allow himself to be pressed into serving the positive cult. He says that he is a firm believer in affirmative attitudes and is convinced that they are ''supremely important in successful living.'' But he is quick to add: ''Affirmatives alone are not enough. This world is full of hope and joy, but it is also beset by evil, immorality and sin. You can't say 'Yes' to these things, or even 'Maybe.' You have to say 'No!' and you have to make it stick.''

Happily, most farmers—and most rural Americans—haven't succumbed to the myth that there is a magical way by which governments can create prosperity and high standards of living by either ignoring or flouting economic laws.

Instead of embarking on a political safari in search of the pot of gold that is supposed to be found at the end of the socialist rainbow, we favor building a greater nation, a more appreciative and productive people, and a more responsive community on the rock-ribbed foundation of unparalleled success thus far.

And we do so with an abiding faith that God didn't intend the light of human freedom, nor the private enterprise system so much a part of it, to perish from the earth.

Bibliography

Gardner, Bruce L. *The Governing of Agriculture*, Published for The International Center for Economic Policy Studies and The Institute for the Study of Market Agriculture. Lawrence: The Regents Press of Kansas, 1981.

Nairn, Ronald C. *Wealth of Nations in Crisis*. Houston, Texas 77005: Bayland Publishing (P. O. Box 25386), 1979.

Paarlberg, Don. *Farm and Food Policy: Issues of the 1980s*. Lincoln: University of Nebraska Press, 1980.

Peterson, William H. *The Great Farm Problem*. Chicago: Henry Regnery Co., 1959.

Rydenfelt, Sven. *A Pattern for Failure: Socialist Economies in Crisis*. New York: Harcourt Brace Jovanovich, 1984.

Stroup, Richard L. and Baden, John A. *Natural Resources: Bureaucratic Myths and Environmental Management*. San Francisco: Pacific Institute for Public Policy Research, 1983.

About the Foundation for Economic Education

The Foundation for Economic Education, founded in 1946 by Leonard E. Read, exists to serve individuals concerned about freedom. Recognizing that the real reasons for freedom are grasped only through an understanding of the free market, private property, limited government way of life, The Foundation is a first-source institution providing literature and activities presenting this point of view.

● *The Freeman*, a monthly study journal of ideas on liberty, has been published by the Foundation since 1956. Its articles and essays offer timeless ideas on the positive case for human liberty and criticisms of the failures of collectivism. *The Freeman* is available to anyone upon request. (The extra costs of mailing to any foreign address require a minimum charge of $10.00 per year.)

● Our annual catalogue, *A Literature of Freedom*, carries a wide range of books and audio cassette tapes on a variety of topics related to the freedom philosophy. More than 120 volumes are currently available from the Foundation.

● FEE's seminar program is designed to bring individuals together to better understand and communicate free market ideas. In addition to three week-long seminars at FEE each summer, several one- and two-day sessions are offered at FEE and at different locations in the United States. The seminar faculty, composed of FEE staff members and guest lecturers, cover economic, philosophical, and historical topics. Discussion sessions provide valuable opportunities to question and explore ideas.

● High school and college students. We actively encourage the study of free market ideas in high schools and colleges in a number of different ways:

On-campus lectures by FEE staff members. Groups vary in size from small classes to school-wide assemblies. Lectures are always followed by a question and answer session.

Seminars in Irvington. Each year FEE hosts three weekend seminars for selected undergraduates from around the nation. These seminars present a solid introduction to free market economics and the philosophy of limited government and individual responsibility.

Debate materials. FEE assists high school debaters by preparing a collection of free market materials covering the current national debate topic. More than 1,000 of these booklets are distributed annually.

Freedom essay contest. An annual competition for students with cash awards for winners. Prize-winning essays are published in *The Freeman*.

For a student subscription to *The Freeman,* or to inquire about any of our other student programs, please write to FEE.

The costs of *The Freeman* and other FEE projects are met through tax-deductible donations. The financial support of more than 12,000 individuals permits the Foundation to distribute its publications widely and to advance the prospects for freedom in America. Join us in this important work!

For further information, write:

The Foundation for Economic Education, Inc.
Irvington-on-Hudson, New York 10533